Unlikely
People

Unlikely People

REESE PALLEY

SHERIDAN HOUSE

First published 1998 by
Sheridan House Inc.
145 Palisade Street
Dobbs Ferry, NY 10522

Library of Congress Cataloging-in-Publication Data
Palley, Reese.
    Unlikely people / Reese Palley.
        p.   cm.
    ISBN 1-57409-057-7 (alk. paper)
    1. Sailors—Biography.   2. Sailing—Miscellanea.   3. Palley,
Reese.   I. Title.
GV810.9.P35   1998
797.1'24—dc21   98-39617
                                                                         CIP

Editor: Janine Simon
Designer: Jeremiah B. Lighter

Cover photo: Marilyn Arnold Palley

Printed in the United States of America

ISBN   1-57409-057-7

This book is for my brother Norman.
However inadequate a dedication may be,
I know of no better way to repay him.

Contents

UNLIKELY PEOPLE Being a report on the strange, wonderful and altogether unlikely folk the writer met in the course of a 20-year circumnavigation of the globe.

Argument

THE WORLD IS MADE UP of fools and philosophers, se-
ducers and seers, and all degrees in between. We
have them all about us on land; and because of the
endless presence of all sorts of folk about us we often fail
to appreciate the good, denigrate the bad, cry with the sad,
and laugh with those who leaven our lot with the human
comedy.

There are too many of them on land to sort out and,
anyway, we are inured to their uniqueness by their
madding presence. You need distance from our crowded
world to really appreciate the panoply of humanity with
which we were blessed and cursed. The best distancing I
know is to go asailing across a great sea.

When you take to the sea in a small boat the absence
of crowding folk tickles your lonely bone so that, when
nifty and not so nifty characters emerge from the fog of
foreign ports, you look at them with eyes popping fresh.
People who would be dimly perceived as without interest
when you lie amidst the tumult of your life ashore, leap
out in delicious clarity.

Indeed this might be the very best reason for taking to
the seas. What greater gift can you give yourself than to
see and feel wonder again as you did when as a child
everything was new, everything was interesting, and everything was worth the note.

In the course of 30 years at sea and two decades of a

circumnavigation, we on UNLIKELY have come across the most unlikely of folk, made even more so by the paucity of contact imposed upon sailors by their separation from the land. In this book we have distilled out not the most outrageous or even the most interesting, but those who, to us, were the most human.

We have sorted out those who are most like all the rest of us . . . some part devil and some part saint. We have avoided the really evil people except in those cases when the Gods, using Odysseus' shield, have returned evil to the evil doer. There is really nothing more satisfying than a bit of heavenly justice.

CHAPTER ONE
Funny People

SOME FOLK HAVE EARNED their way into this book, advertently or inadvertently, because they tickle the funny bone. Most are sailors in this chapter whose droll events chronicled here lightened the sometime overwhelming task of pushing a small sailboat around the world.

The funny people are situated first in the book because those who make us laugh are the most treasured gift of humanity. I still chuckle at the stockbroker's tip, laugh uproariously at irrepressible Willie, and smile when I think of the Myajima man. You will too.

WILLIE

I was once diverted, by the ill winds of flu and chance, to sail into the country of Colombia at a port called Buenaventura which, in spite of its salubrious name, is the nethermost orifice of the universe.

Upon entering Buenaventura I was beset by a small, elderly, and entirely disreputable looking ragamuffin who called himself Willie. He claimed to be an American citizen whose papers had mysteriously disappeared. Willie offered all sorts of services (it being Colombia the menu was large) in exchange for what he claimed was a modest fee. I felt sure he was hustling me and could not produce half of what he promised, so I turned him coldly away. Besides, he was altogether too ratty looking to represent me to the authorities.

As befitting a proper skipper of a proper yacht, I sought out the official route and made my way to a glorious luminary, the door of whose office proclaimed him *Captain of the Port*. His office was draped with Colombian flags and speckled with noble photographs of everyone in Colombia who was at least one step above him in the hierarchy. He was taking no chances. I was courteously received. I explained that I had diverted into Buenaventura due to an illness aboard. I needed a physician and would be on my way in a day or two.

There was much sympathy expressed for a *hermano norte americano*. A physician was summoned and I was told that I would be put into the hands of the captain's best agent, a man of high probity who could "make all things possible for me." As I departed I grew an inch or two in my own self-esteem.

I soon discovered that the captain of the port had only recently purchased his warrant and was intent on recouping his entire investment from the first Yankee sailboat owner to fall into his grasp. Namely, me.

When the recommended agent (the captain's brother-in-law, as it turned out) visited my boat the next day, he apologetically informed me that there would be a "few minor, unavoidable charges too insignificant to discuss" and which certainly would be no financial burden for the owner of so splendid a vessel as mine.

I smelled a rat.

Before the agent departed my boat I pressed him for the exact extent of the 'insignificant' charges. He urged me to wait till I was ready to leave so that he could best arrange matters. The rat got smellier and when I insisted he guessed that it would be, "Uh . . . huh . . . not really much more than, all told mind you, not much more than $2,000 a day."

The tale of my escape from the mulcting clutches of the captain of the port will be told elsewhere but when later I complained to Willie he drew himself up to his full, bedraggled five feet and said, "Señor, a thousand pardons, but you are *un santo inocente*. I required only a little of your money, those bastards want it all!"

For the rest of my stay in Buenaventura I hired Willie to be my guide, mentor, and deck guard. His ancient and shaky physique, even if he were healthy (he was not) and even if he were strong (he could hardly haul himself on deck), was no match for the hulking cutthroats who hovered about the fringes on my vessel. However I felt that I had done poor Willie an injustice. I owed him the job. He could use the money and, as he explained, he could use the *oportunidad* that went along with his position as amanuensis to the American yacht.

I had been warned by friends that if I did not submit to the cozenage and peculation of the *official* pirates I would be descended upon nightly and stripped clean by harbor thieves in the pay of officialdom. Since there was no way that I could afford to play the captain of the port's extortionist game, I had resigned myself to pillage by the harbor thugs who were hourly edging closer, and hired Willie as a last measure.

Within moments after Willie came aboard the tightening circle of light-fingered gentry receded like a fast ebbing tide and, by the next day, the hovering had ceased entirely. Indeed, small boats in the harbor went to extreme measures to detour around us at a great distance and at the cost of much additional labor on their part. I watched Willie closely for some hint of his magic. All he seemed to do was lie about on deck, coughing a bit, as was his wont, and looking smug.

We had to stay a week in that terrible place but we

were as safe as in our mother's arms. No one bothered us. No one approached us. No one, and this is incredible, even tried to beg from us. We were surrounded by Willie's mysterious force field.

When the time came to leave I grossly overpaid Willie and asked what he had done to intimidate the entire harbor. Willie, being no fool, smiled slyly, refused to divulge his secret and suggested that I advise all my American friends to seek him out for protection. I swore I would.

We cleared both customs and the police, with unseemly haste on their part. It was evident that they wanted us the hell out of their harbor. We waved goodbye to Willie and sailed out.

About a mile off the coast, still in Colombian waters, the entire Colombian Navy, or so it seemed, descended upon us and, with guns trained, ordered us to stop for a search. We thought it was a belated look-see for cocaine and since we were as clean of drugs as Nancy Reagan's medicine chest, we welcomed them aboard . . . not that we had much choice.

The search was thorough. Twenty armed Colombian marines herded us onto the foredeck and, with exaggerated care, left no possible hiding place unplumbed. Four hours later they trooped back to their ships, obviously relieved that their search had turned up nothing.

The whole episode was an unfathomable puzzle for me until, as the last Colombian sailor climbed aboard his boat, I heard him report to his officer,

"*Willie está loco. Los Americanos no tienen una bomba atómica*".

God bless Willie and never underestimate the threat of nuclear Armageddon.

THE MYAJIMA MAN

Even though we arrived with the first ooze of dawn, the Miyajima man was waiting for us at dockside. He was dressed for a regatta. White, rubber-soled, leather shoes, creamy trousers with creases sharp and precise, a perfect, double-breasted blue blazer dotted with bright gold buttons and a hat braided as for the admiral of the Queen's Navy. We later learned that the buttons were solid gold, a gift from his respectful and adoring (and dependent) employees. We were also to learn much about respect and the Japanese cult of gift giving from the Miyajima man.

Since this was the southernmost of the Japanese islands and we were flying our Q flag, he formally welcomed us to Japan as representative, commodore actually, of the MYJ, the Myajima Yacht Club. He asked if he might come aboard. When he sat on the dock, after spreading a perfect white silk scarf to preserve his trousers, and removed his shoes and his socks, we recognized him as a real sailor. No sailor would try to negotiate a new deck in sock clad feet. This would be dangerous and anyway, as we were to learn from the Japanese compulsion for ablutions, his feet were as clean as the early snows of winter.

He cocked a critical eye at gear and mast and sails. In a very good English he made some insightful, though politely arch, comments concerning our rigging and congratulated us on missing the typhoons which were whirling about between Guam and Japan.

The name of our boat, UNLIKELY, stopped him cold. "Unrucky?" he asked, "surely not the best name for a sailboat."

No, no, we assured him, not Unlucky, Unlikely. It was a word with which he was not familiar. An improbable event, we explained, something which surprised, in our case, pleasantly.

He lit up with laughter and for the year that we remained in Japan, the boat's name evoked more merriment in this reserved land than anything else that we had brought to them. After much consultation with the English teachers at the local school (learning English is an obligation in Japan—as are most other things) he had the word translated into Japanese, gold leafed onto a sign which we hung a little shyly on the portside spreaders. It was just one of many gifts which were to raise both our waterline and our consciousness of how wide the cultural gulf is between them and us.

For the first few days he was distant and proper. He was energetic in keeping others off our boat. "They would be a bother . . . not sailors," he explained. He gathered us in, oiled the way, dealt with officials, paid our dock fees without telling us and, three times a day, brought us gifts. We found it curious that he had arranged for us to remain at the public dock rather than at his yacht club but it was a location that we came to prefer since shopping and victualing were much easier.

On the third day he brought a friend, on the fourth three friends, and by week's end he was conducting tours of our boat for privileged and carefully selected 'friends' of Myajima. His entourage was always polite and careful. They asked few questions of us but said "Ah so" a lot to the Myajima man. We had gradually, imperceptibly, been acquired.

There is no such thing as equality in Japan. There is a shade, a mere tint of difference, between each Japanese. It is neither a great honor to be superior nor a great shame to be inferior. That is just the way it is. The Myajima man was demonstrably superior to any of the folk he brought aboard. Perhaps they were all carefully pre-selected to be below him on the pecking order but, in any event, they treated him very carefully indeed. We were clucked over, and given presents, but it was the Myajima man who commanded their attention.

The Myajima man announced, with a touch of *no-*

blesse oblige, that he would be bringing a group of friends from the yacht club on Sunday for a little sail around the bay. They were, he said, in great anticipation of the event.

When they arrived on Sunday there were twenty five of them, a burden for our vessel but we made do. They carried cameras like a contingent of Japanese tourists in Hawaii and the Myajima man had a video camera, a rare curiosity at the time.

There was a great to-do concerning the upcoming sail. The excitement was intense as they spread themselves elegantly around the deck, photo recording everything in sight. As members of the yacht club they were all properly, identically, turned out in blue and white. Each wore a large, plastic, commemorative button with the legend, *The Myajima Yacht Club Unlikely Cruise*! It seemed like an awful lot for a couple of hours in the bay.

The day went extremely well. The Myajima man assumed the helm as if it were his right and due. We had sun, a brisk wind, much eating and drinking and even a little squall toward the end to spice up matters. The *Myajima Yacht Club Unlikely Cruise* was a huge success as evidenced by the inordinate amount of gift giving that took place. Over the next few days we received enough Japanese dolls and exquisitely wrapped Japanese candies to take care of our trade goods' needs for months. The Philippinos, in our next port, loved the dolls.

But, we remained puzzled over the passion and excitement of a few hours on the bay—especially for such elegantly turned out yacht club members. They were not exaggerating their delight. It was evident that the episode was something special which had been arranged for them by the Myajima man. When I complained to him of the excessive volume of gifts he hinted at a similar problem.

Later we pulled into the Kobe Yacht Club on the mainland where Aosoki San, a lean and leathery *roué* of advanced age and prurient interest in young Japanese school girls, hosted us in a more reserved manner than had the Myajima man. Aosoki San was a tough old sailor who ran the club, his own 36 footer, and a clutch of gigglers (in Japan young girls giggle a lot) with an efficient and iron hand.

In the course of our stay at the club, where everything was free, we got to talking about Myajima. We showed Aosoki our commemorative button and asked why sailors would have made such a fuss over so small a matter.

"The Myajima Yacht Club," he explained, "is only twenty years old. Their membership is growing and all have passed the strict written exams for a sailing license. They are quite proper," and here he groped for a word, "yachtsmen. Unfortunately they are still in the planning stage for a club house and facilities and, of course, as yet, none of them have boats."

So that's why the excitement. Our friends had assumed the stance of yachtsmen in the clothing and accouterment of western sailors. It explained much of the ability of the Japanese to ingest foreign technologies and mores.

It also explained why, on every Sunday throughout our stay in Japan, we would see crowds of sportily turned out golfers going to and fro on the streets, carrying clubs in expensive bags.

But we never did run across a golf course.

HOW TONY GOT RICH

What follows is a secret which I had sworn never to tell. But the tale is too good to hoard and, anyway, Tony is probably long gone.

I was in London shortly after World War II, at a time when the English were impoverished and denied most of the luxury foods to which at least the upper classes had been accustomed.

Any offer of foods that were even mildly reminiscent of the gustatory past were greedily sought. In that land of horse lovers, even horse meat, carefully hidden behind a French menu, was a treat.

So it was not surprising that a small pub in Chelsea was developing a strong following among the cognoscenti because of the special edible treat that was offered. The pub was owned by an Italian who had been a prisoner of war and who had elected to stay in Britain. Tony complained endlessly about the cold and the damp and yearned for his native Napoli but because his business was thronged with hungry Englishmen seeking his forbidden delicacy, he hung on in Chelsea.

The delicacy was caviar, black caviar which, even before the war, was sold by the precious ounce. Tony's ploy was that each evening at five o'clock, he would place on the bar a huge mound of black caviar which was offered free with no limits to all of his imbibing patrons. All you had to do was buy a beer.

We all wondered how Tony could afford what was hundreds of dollars worth of caviar in exchange for a few pennyworth of beers. Many inquired but Tony's only response was to advise his clients, "*Mangia, mangia*, stop worrying, enjoy, enjoy."

Some believed that Tony was a millionaire black marketer, and some thought that he was just plain crazy, but all of us continued to wolf down Tony's caviar. If a heap became depleted another appeared instantly.

This went on for some years as his business grew apace. The time came when Tony announced that his yearning for Napoli was too great and that he was closing the pub and leaving. There was much mourning.

We all tried to learn his secret caviar source but to all inquiries Tony gave an enormous Italian wink and a firm, but polite refusal.

I had become a special friend during the years I was in London since I was his only friend who could get bourbon from the American Embassy. On the night of Tony's departure I made a final effort. I stopped at the embassy and blew a month's allowance on his favorite, Jim Beam. Tony was sad and lachrymose at leaving and full of conflicting Latin emotions. I helped his mood by arranging that he also be full of Jim Beam, no less rare than his caviar.

After closing, we sat in the now shuttered pub and I ladled the liquor down Tony's throat. He became an emotional puddle and when, finally, I pressed him for his great secret Tony, in an alcoholic stupor, gave in.

"I shall share my great secret with only you," he wept, "but you must swear to never reveal it."

I swore and this is the tale he told.

"It is simple, my friend, as all great ideas are simple. I was no black marketer and I am only crazy like a fox."

I pressed him, fearful that he should pass out with the great secret unrevealed.

"So, you boil up a mess of tapioca, lace it with loads of anchovy paste and color it black with a food dye and presto," he winked his enormous wink, "you have caviar!"

All of the years that I had been eating Tony's 'caviar', I had been convinced that his was by far the best caviar I had ever eaten.

Now I knew why.

THE WORLD'S DUMBEST SAILOR

The dumbest man I ever knew pulled in next to me in the Larnaca marina on the troubled island of Cyprus. We were nicely docked on the north pier along with a clutch of congenial sailors. We were very much aware, especially we

Americans, of the proximity to Cyprus of the ruined country of Lebanon, just one day's sail to the east of us. To the northeast was unstable and unpredictable Syria. To the southeast was Israel, besieged by the stone throwers, and worse, of the West Bank.

It was the proper moment to resist flaunting pride of country. It was a time to avoid becoming a target for the general frustrations of the Palestinians. It was a time to recognize that fundamentalist Arabs believed the best way to get to heaven quickly was to die in a shoot out with an infidel.

When Lebanon went up in flames, much of the skullduggery that was its daily fare shifted to Cyprus. The Cypriots publicly claimed disgust, but the cash flowed and oiled away opposition. Cyprus became the setting for every James Bondish adventure imaginable. In the midst of a surge of tourism, of which the yachting portion was not insignificant, bombs, highjacking, murder, and the buying and selling of state secrets competed with the buying and selling of drugs. An altogether intimidating atmosphere for a passel of American yachties, most of whom had only recently escaped from the intimidations, political and natural, of the Red Sea.

It was the time and the place for the most extreme circumspection.

Into this setting chugs the *World's Dumbest Sailor*. He came over from Lebanon, flying a Lebanese flag, accompanied by a high-heeled, flounced and satined bimbo. His boat was about thirty feet of undistinguished cabin cruiser and after he settled in next to me, he called over,

"Atlantic City, eh?"

"Yessiree," I answered. I was a bit nervous at being identified as an enemy of the Ayatollah but the big black letters on my transom brooked little dissimulation.

"How long ya been out?" he asked and it dawned on me that this was no denizen of the Mideast. This was a genuine, born in the U.S.A., American. His accent left no doubt. No need to ask him who pitched that perfect game for the Dodgers. I felt a bit better.

" 'Bout nine years," I said with a touch of preen.

"I been out a lot longer."

Now there are damn few sailors, especially American sailors, who have been out a bit, let alone a lot, longer than nine years and even fewer who chose to spend those years in a small cabin cruiser. My curiosity was piqued.

"Whatchya been doin'?"

And here the world's dumbest sailor earned his title. In a loud voice that carried, I was sure, into every terrorist nest on this infested island, he declared,

"Oh, I work for the State Department in Beirut."

A kind of silence settled over the marina. The wind dropped, the halyards stopped clanking, and every head turned to make sure they had heard right. A slight titter of amused surprise floated like a small wave through the assembled boats. A U.S. State Department man announcing it loudly? In Cyprus? Disbelief ran high. Disbelief accompanied by suppressed laughter at his stupidity. Had he not seen the photo of the murdered Israeli lady hanging dead, in her nightgown, over the pulpit of her sailboat moored in this very marina? Had he not followed on television just the previous month the peregrinations of the hijacked Kuwaiti 747? Or the bombings? Or the kidnapping by the Mossad of a high PLO official from a spot not ten yards from where the world's dumbest sailor was docking his boat? This was not a matter for wonder . . . this was a matter for laughter.

The only thing I could manage to say, swallowing a guffaw and struck almost mute by his gratuitous revelation, was a nervous:

"Uh, yeh, huh. Pretty risky, eh?"

"Could be. Pretty stupid to hang around there, I guess."

I could not help but agree. I did not add that the only

thing riskier than working for the U.S. Department of State in Lebanon was to dumbly announce it in Cyprus. I did not think that he would understand. I started to plan how I was going to justify a new dock as far away from this madman as I could get. I could hear every phone on the island relaying with ill-concealed amusement the exciting news that a prime target, and a particularly identifiable one, had popped up like a gift from Allah. I wanted to be away from him lest I become an accidental ticket to paradise for some passionate Shi'ite.

At this juncture, the scenario becomes more farcical as three swarthy Cypriot gunsels appeared. To my relief they were greeted by our sailor as friends into whose care he left his boat. A black limousine appeared as by magic, festooned, if you will believe it, with American flags. Off he went with his lady to do who knows what other dumb stuff on an island that was clearly bad for his health. He left the gunsels who, I learned, could not be bought but could be rented, standing guard. I was denied a different berth and for the next three days I watched ever more curious types meander down the north pier, a place that had attracted little attention prior to his arrival.

My curiosity held me past my intended departure time, anchored in this mideastern OK Corral by a need to watch the lethal comedy work itself out. The only thing that might save the world's dumbest sailor, I reasoned, was that the Shi'ites were probably dumber than he.

See you in the headlines.

* * *

The only excuses for including the following two characters is that it tells the reader a bit about where I came from and what occupied me before I went to sea.

Both of these events took place while I was still peddling fine art, objects of art, and just plain kitsch on the boardwalk in Atlantic City. In the twenty years during which I paraded up and down my own retail stage abusing and amusing my 'pigeons', there were just as many funny, good, bad, and remarkable people in those landed years as there were later at sea. But that is another book. Here are two of the best.

THE STOCKBROKER

He was not quite as round as he was tall but he carried about him a palpable aura of authority. More than that, it was the sense that the authority he exuded derived not from normal wellsprings of knowledge and wisdom, open to all men, but from covert and arcane sources available only to those who were born and bred to the New York Stock Exchange.

The Exchange had been his home from the day he emerged, *sans* diploma, from his second year at New York University. He would later opine that wisdom was a commodity that could be bought while money had to be truly earned.

And truly earn it he did. By the time World War II came around he had inserted himself into the prized and wildly lucrative position of NYSE sugar specialist to an America which was being squeezed of its sugar by the war effort.

His life proved his argument since he was demonstrably not wise but he certainly was rich. And the lesson he taught me was so obvious and so blindingly simple that it astounds me to this day that it is not the first lecture of 'How To Succeed 101'.

"How did you become so rich?" I asked one day after I discovered that the word 'rich' to my friend was not a four letter word. "How so much, how so soon and why you?"

My friend paused for a moment. I later learned that the pause was not to organize his thoughts about what he was going to say, but rather to decide whether or not he should share valuable information with me. His affection for me overcame his reluctance to allow anyone else but himself an advantage.

After a very long pause he asked a curious question, "What happens when you make a phone call and say nothing?"

"I suppose people hang up."

"No," said the stockbroker, "not right away. They will stay on the line for a bit and continue to talk to whoever was in their room when the phone rang."

"Yes, so?" I answered very much in the dark.

"Well, Sir, in my business, where people talk all of the time and where information is what divides the rich from the poor, a good part of my success is this."

The stockbroker paused, glanced around, and in a lowered voice said,

"When I make a call I pause for a few seconds and listen. It is astounding what precious information people will pass into a 'dead' phone. I got very, very rich on dead air."

THE JUNK DEALER

As it turned out, he was the sweetest man I ever met. Not that his appearance, that day when he came into my shop, foreshadowed my affection for him.

He was small and round with the satisfied roundness of acquired, not genetic, poundage. He was badly dressed but not so egregiously as his wife who was also short and carried more weight than her frame allowed.

Our place was fancy, catering mostly to upreachers who were beginning, self-consciously, to enjoy the fruits of the first rich decade after World War II. It was an expensive, exquisitely appointed shop, perfectly suited to folk who, while not born to taste, were hell bent on acquiring some.

It was the best of times . . . for a retailer who knew just one syllable more than his clients. It was a time to rake it in from trusting, yearning folk who themselves had been raking it in and who wanted, by their purchases from us, to haul themselves one more step up the ladder.

The junk dealer strode quietly about the shop, smoking a long and black cigar as his wife sorted through our English bone china collection. She was dressed in the mode of wartime America, a stiff boxy suit, stuffed with sharp shoulder pads. She was shod in klutzy shoes not yet imported from Italy.

She wore clusters of pink gold jewelry set with milky rubies and almost emeralds. She was right out of the civilian side of World War II. She was the perfect pigeon for a shop such as ours.

I began to worry as I watched her instinctively hone in on our most expensive tableware. She needed, she said, something 'drop dead' to ease her way above her peers. Her taste was indelicate, which matched, strangely, the most expensive that English bone china had to offer, the Imari patterns by Royal Crown Derby.

Surveying her oldish clothes and inexpensive jewelry I sensed that the day would be wasted unless I could edge her into something more suited to what I assumed was her purse. I had long since learned that a retailer tries at his risk to impose his will on a woman in passionate pursuit of class. Any mention of price would have dashed the lovely euphoria she was in and would, I was sure, lose me an important sale.

So I quietly took the junk dealer aside.

"Sir," I said, "your wife seems to be settling on a most expensive pattern and we do not want to embarrass her when she is told the price."

The junk dealer glanced over at his wife, took the cigar out of his mouth and delicately tapped the ashes onto his protruding shirt front.

He paused for a moment, smiled and as he glanced fondly at his wife he said,

"Think nothing of it . . . we're newly rich."

CHAPTER TWO

Good People

T HEY CAN BE RARER then you can ever imagine and are not nearly as much fun as funny people. However, compared to non-sailors, folk who take to the sea tend on the average to be more good than bad. Possibly it is because in rejecting the restive, troubled, and raggedy world of land, sailors have not had all of the good yet squeezed out of them.

Besides, they are our salvation. It is written in an ancient tome that as long as there are 48 truly good people on earth we are safe from destruction.

We met half of these blessed 48 at sea. To select a few out of the many we met around the globe is not fair. Most of the good folk we met have been worthy of at least one star. Those included here have earned, like a great restaurant, three.

A LESSON IN VIRTUE

The Virtue came in under full sail, no engine, and no one on the foredeck. Only the helmsman could be seen. The little boat sailed quietly through the cluttered pack, picking her way among the lumbering charters, and swung around sharply into the wind in a small clear area far from the herd. She stopped dead as a sailboat must when brought into the wind. The helmsman crawled creakily out of the cockpit and, in an old man's hobble, limped to the bow where his rode had already been flaked out. He silently paid out and put his hook into the harbor bottom. He slowly (for he was a very old man and could do little quickly) took down his main and bagged his jib while the Virtue was finding her natural lay. The whole process took about ten minutes and was accomplished without a sound. The old man softly called up his equally ancient wife to stand anchor watch, and then he disappeared below, from which he reappeared eight hours later refreshed by a sound nap.

From this little dance, a soft shoe shuffle by an old man approaching his eighties, I learned that an entrance into harbor need not be, nay must not be, achieved in the shrill tones of panic and dismay. The old man knew his boat, knew her habits, knew the harbor, and had carefully prepared for anchoring. All went as well for him as it usually went badly for me and I decided to stop charging full ahead and to start learning. The elegant ancient was Sir Humphrey Barton, admiral of the Ocean Cruising Club, crosser of big oceans in small Virtues. The admiral had something I wanted.

I didn't know who he was that day in the harbor of Tortola, in the British Virgin Islands, but I went acalling anyway. He, and his lady, welcomed me graciously aboard a tiny boat (this was his seventeenth Atlantic crossing) neat as a pin and salty as a herring. It was all warm, dark wood, and laden with books where today we might be overladen with electronics. We talked about the elegance of his entrance and the disasters of mine. He assured me that it was no disgrace to be a beginner. The only disgrace was to remain a beginner.

From Sir Humphrey Barton I ultimately learned that

a good entrance into any port is no accident. It is a product of thought, judgment, and experience. "An elegant entrance," the admiral told me, "is when you arrive with the least possible effort and," he added with a wry smile, "a perfectly elegant entrance is when you do it with no effort at all."

I have spent decades since seeking the 'perfectly elegant' entrance. I have learned to accept a 'fender bender' touch on another boat, of which only two parties are aware, rather than the screams of warning which broadcast my ineptitude to the entire anchored fleet.

I have learned to do a snail-slow entrance and not to rely on my noisy engine which is most likely to fail at the end of a sea passage. Sails do not fail and mark the newcomer as a sailor indeed.

I have learned to flake out my anchor rode and to assiduously avoid stepping into a coil as the anchor goes out.

And I have learned one of the laws of sailing.

He who flakes out his rode and then stands not an anchor watch is a flake of a different color.

Make your mistakes at sea which is forgiving of the tyro and where no one is looking or judging. Lest you be judged inept and unsalty by your peers, commit no errors in harbor.

And always watch carefully how the really old guys do it as they have neither the strength nor the agility to deal with crises. But, lacking both, they have the most valuable sailorly talent of all—experience.

DAVID AND THE KALASHNIKOV

It all started with blue-eyed Ellie.

Blue-eyed Ellie was born in Poland in the wrong year and to the wrong parents. He lived out the war, in terror and in hiding, in occupied France. He ultimately became respected and successful in the academic world but he never lost his talent for caution or his instinct for survival and self protection.

Blue-eyed Ellie finally emigrated from his beloved France to Israel for reasons not even altogether clear to himself. I found him there hammering away at an old iron boat. I came to love Ellie, as did everyone. He had retired from the university and was, at 60, preparing for ocean passages. When, half in jest, I asked him to sail with me down the Red Sea and on toward Australia, his caution and conservatism fled him and, to my surprise, to his surprise, and to the collective surprise of all who knew of his passion for remaining out of harm's way, he instantly agreed.

Blue-eyed Ellie stood by his commitment although he soon was overwhelmed with the need to make the passage as safe as possible. He appointed himself navigator and planned precise passages to minutes on the clock and cables in the sea. He appointed himself rigger and, though over 60, he clambered and climbed about the rigging, supple as a bamboo shoot, in a frenzy of inspection. He had become plucky, but not foolish. He was covering his cautious French *derrière*.

But this yarn is not about blue-eyed Ellie, though it well could be. It is about David, his friend, and it is about the most inappropriate task ever laid on me.

In his passion for anticipating any possible upcoming confront, blue-eyed Ellie asked to see my arms' chest. He was unimpressed with my ancient shotgun. What I needed, this small and civilized and gentle Frenchman declared, was a serious weapon, something fully automatic with which I could protect us in the Red Sea when the Arab fanatics would come for his carefully preserved Israeli hide. I was appointed gunsel for Ellie.

Automatic weapons cannot be bought in Israel but blue-eyed Ellie had a friend who had a Kalashnikov rifle, an AK47, the best and most terrible automatic weapon ever built. He was intent that his friend loan it to us. But the friend, David, had a problem. David, having fought effectively in every Israeli war since 1947, had evolved into a passionate pacifist. He could not any longer live with the thought that any gun of his might be used in a warlike manner. And how else can one use a Kalashnikov?

On the other hand, in the best Talmudic tradition, David agonized over his responsibility to us lest we sail off without the Kalashnikov and be set upon by savage hordes. Ultimately he gave in to his need to see us 'protected'. He presented me with the Kalashnikov and, at the same time, made a nice little rabbinic suggestion which got him neatly off the pointy horns of his dilemma.

"I give you this weapon of war which is intended to kill and maim my fellow man," David formally declared. "I give it to you upon the condition that, although it is a weapon of war, you must find a peaceful use for it."

Now I ask you, how do you find a peaceful use for a gun that never jams, will empty a fifty-round clip in seconds, and was designed, specifically, to cut a man in half? I accepted the weapon for nervous Ellie's sake and with crossed fingers accepted David's charge that I discover a peaceful use. Ha!

We sailed off from Israel, headed down through the Suez Canal. In the Red Sea, between Yemen and Ethiopia—a harder rock and a harder place would be impossible to find—our mast broke off at twenty feet above deck. It hung by its internal wires and cables and halyards from the remaining stub, banging merrily against our hull to the tune of an unpleasant sea. The hanging mast section had to come down lest it do us further damage. There was, however, no way to send anyone aloft to cut it down lest the cut away mast and flailing cables remove some part of the person doing the cutting. A dilemma indeed.

I pondered the matter and hit upon a scheme that solved both my immediate, dangerous dilemma and David's moral one. I went below, shoved a full clip into David's Kalashnikov, came on deck, braced myself, switched the gun to full automatic and blazed away at the offending cables. It only took a second and the mast slid quietly into the sea. The Kalashnikov, like a giant pair of scissors, had sheared them away.

My mast was in the sea. My dilemma was solved. And, against all odds, I had obeyed David's injunction to find a "peaceful use" for his murderous gun.

In the Red Sea, as ancient history teaches, anything can happen.

DON WINDSOR OF GALLE

In Sri Lanka, known in a more civilized age by the euphonious name of Ceylon, there is a small harbor. It lies on the south coast of the fragrant isle and its name is Galle (rhymes with Gaul). Galle is no big deal of a harbor. It is tiny and crowded and, for some arcane reason, the Japanese are blowing up the harbor bottom, crazing our gelcoat and commenting explosively, perhaps, on having been nuked in World War II.

The chief harbor is in Colombo, the capital of Sri Lanka. It is busy, unfriendy, and so dirty that it appears diseased. As a result, most cruising sailors seeking shelter after the dash from Singapore or the nasty beat from Cocos Keeling, will head for Galle, or Windsor Country, as it has become known.

Windsor Country does not refer to the British royal family, but rather to Don Windsor, entrepeneur extraordinaire, defender of widows and orphans, and builder of Buddhas. And, we must hasten to add, a world class commission man.

There is a story that is told in this Isle of Serendip-
ity—the original rulers of old Ceylon were called the
Princes of Serendip—which every cruising sailor is required to hear at least once. And although it may be apoc-
ryphal and certainly is not complimentery to its
protagonist, if no one else will tell you, then Don Windsor
himself will make sure that you do not miss it. Don Windsor, you see, loves the sound of his name, no matter what
is being said of him.

The tale describes a trio of savants wiling away a
lifetime or two, enlarging on the beasts which God had
placed in such profusion upon the earth. The three wise
men were each straining, as wise men do, to out-savant
the other.

The first wise man said, "The most wonderous
beast, with certainly the most exquisitely honed talent,
must be the shark. A single drop of blood dripped into
ten thousand *lahks* of sea water will suffice to bring the
shark swiftly. What a glory to God is such a miraculous
faculty!"

The second wise man, a little older and perforce a
little wiser, snorted derisively as wise men often do and
said, "Bah! A trick of chemistry, not wonderful at all,
too easily explained. Certainly the Lord is more subtle
than that. Consider instead the vulture and how that curious and prescient bird sees into the future. From the
very door of the heavens the vulture is aware, even before his arrival, of the coming of the terrible Angel of
Death. Not even the wisest among us (and I modestly include myself) can predict where Death will strike and yet
the vulture is always at hand to greet Him. What a
mystery!"

The third ancient, a holy man of the most extreme
age, with the experience of ten reincarnations, tightened
his lotus, and wheezed, "Mystery? What mystery? Alti-
tude and acuity, that is all. To appreciate the depths and
the pinnacles of the miracles that God has put on this

earth, do not look to the stupid shark or the voracious vulture. Look instead to an awesome being shrouded in beauty and drenched in wisdom. Look and be amazed at the harrowing powers," and here his voice dropped in reverence (or perhaps in the ancient fear of the Name calling up the Being), "of Don Windsor. At the merest rustle of a rupee, far out across the waters and deep in the pocket of an unsuspecting sailor, Windsor can extract his ten percent, long before the sailor even sights the port of Galle. For awesome powers and proof of the glory of God, look then to Don Windsor of Galle, smeller of rupees, extractor of commissions, and friend of the working sailor."

To be able to extract a commission when the extractee is not even aware of the deed is a great talent. But in truth (which is, alas, oftentimes less interesting than fiction) the talents and abilities of Don Windsor, Grand Mufti of Galle, serve the cruising sailor remarkably well even as his pocket is being lightened. As an extractor of commissions, Don may well be subtle and effective, but he cannot approach the avarice of some others whose paths and palms I have crossed in my travels. In Sri Lanka, as in most of the dingier corners of the third world, there is always some bastard who is dissatisfied with a tenth or a fifth, he wants it all. If you should find yourself cruising the benighted coasts of the third world and happen upon a commission man satisfied with a reasonable slice of your cash, hire him, woo him, and make of him your friend, for there are many worse waiting in the wings.

Granted that Don Windsor takes. But he also gives value for payment. From the moment you arrive in Galle till the moment you leave, you belong to Don, at least ten percent of you does. For every service, from rinsing out your dainties to defusing the police, Don gets his piece of the action.

Don Windsor takes, but when big problems overwhelm you, those emergencies and dramas from which all of your closest friends seem to flee, Don doffs his commission man's hat and reveals, in the doffing, a bald pate surrounded by an airy fringe of silky hair which looks like nothing less than the halo he has earned many times over from lending desperately needed assistance, attainable nowhere else in Sri Lanka at any price.

Don Windsor comes through. Even as he is complaining that there is nothing he can do about that special disaster of yours, he is already doing it. "Do not involve me!" he cries as he involves himself. In a part of the world where it is considered childish idiocy to go up against authority of any kind, Don Windsor dons his armor and, like a small brown Lochinvar out of the East, he spills bureaucratic blood by the bucket.

Don is intensely sentimental and his heart is marshmallow soft. He tries desperately to project the image of a money changer in the temple, cold, hard and greedy. But his actions, if not his disclaimers, belie the disguise. Pull aside the veil even slightly, and there stands revealed a serendipitous Wizard of Oz. He boasts of what a terrible fellow he is and how fierce and unconcerned, while in truth and in action he is so deeply involved in the humanism of his Buddha, that he dots the Gallean landscape with expensive images of that lovely lord. For Don is a believer, no small feat in this cynical world of ours. Not satisfied with letting it go with belief, he is the center of most of the secular Buddhism of his province.

All this adds to the direct benefit of the cruising sailor. If Lord Buddha teaches that strangers must be taken in, then Don does so. If Buddha teaches that the stupid and dull among us must be cared for, Don has a special place for them in his heart. And when the Lord Buddha decrees that your neighbors must be treated as you yourself would wish to be treated, then, when Sinhalese are screaming for Tamil blood, Don, at considerable risk, shelters an otherwise helpless Tamil child.

Don Windsor has a soul as pure as the gold he lusts

after. Contradiction and paradox. In his world contradiction and paradox are how things are. In his personality, the spiritual and the material are each so palpably present that he is always a bit out of focus. Just when you have labeled him as a greedy, grasping ten percenter, he gives you a glimpse of what Lord Buddha really meant man to be.

So hooray for Don Windsor, believer, friend and helper. A man of piety and wit who tries not to let you believe a word of it. May Lord Buddha grant that we have more like him to help smooth our sometimes troubled passages in the antipodean ports of this curious world.

GIVE IN

Thirty years ago I was sailing in the British Virgin Islands. I had taken a week off in the first flush of promised, but not yet delivered, financial success. I had brought a woman with me who, in those simple but sexually foggy days, I still thought of as my 'mistress'. We had a marvelous time. I was the indomitable sailor braving the terrible seas of the Sir Francis Drake Channel and she was the pro tempore non-wife of a bad marriage.

We dropped anchor into the clear water of a small, empty bay on Peter Island and, just before sunset, we rowed ashore in search of dinner and diversion. We found dinner in a little shack on the beach sporting a sign a bit larger than the shack itself that proclaimed, 'Eats Here'. Dinner was fresh conch salad marinated in lemon juice and red snapper steaks perfectly undercooked. After dinner we wandered down the beach drawn to jingly music that filled the darkness with the beats of Africa and Rio. We were hearing reggae for the first time. It was still unnamed for us but no less intoxicating for its anonymity.

Approaching 40, I was the successful American male entrepreneur. I was on my way towards what I then defined as 'up'. I was required to be social and public in my business, which predominately dealt with women.

But I could not dance.

If you are a dancer, that sounds like a small matter, but it had dominated my life to an extent that only now, thirty years later, is coming clear. I had bumbled through high school and college where the 'cool cats' were all 'smooth' dancers. I had built my relationships, sparse and mostly unsuccessful, with women by talking them into love and passion. It would have been so much easier, and more pleasant for both of us, if we had danced.

Since we cannot travel down the interrupted roadways of our pasts, the why I was no dancer is not nearly so interesting as what it had done to me. I had been denied rhythm and easy sexuality. I could smell, only distantly, the sweet sweat of the physical release of dance. I was bound in psychic restraints so taut that not even the insistent cadences of the music of my youth could loosen.

The absence of a sense of rhythm almost precludes the ability to steer a sailboat since the cadences of the sea must be dealt with instinctively, from the belly, and not from the mind. But I was so young a sailor it was a lesson that I was still to learn from a very old black man, no sailor he, and his young partner.

The music that had drawn us down the dark beach was coming from a small, roofed-over hall, its sides open to the cool night air. The musicians sat in the center on a shaky platform which, at the insistence of the pounding feet, kept curious time with the music. The dancers swirled to the music, all in one direction, like an evening walk in Leningrad. Now and then they would slump onto the slatted benches that ringed the hall. There was no break in the music. The island musicians were deep into their drums and for them stopping was like dying.

I sat on a bench trying to tap my foot to the music. The tapping went badly. Even a thousand miles from home, at the end of the world where no one could snicker save myself, the bonds were still too tight. My hips remained frozen and the muscles that should have been listening had turned tone deaf.

An old man danced by, older then than I am now, with a young girl in his arms upon whose breasts you could bounce a penny. He was dark with the black of purple. His skin, an undisputed advantage of being black, had that textured depth that comes to old, indestructible black skin. His eyes were drunk with the music and with his young girl. When he turned those eyes on me as he danced past, he missed none of my discomfort, none of my pained restraint. He danced around the room three times, always a bit closer. The last time, brushing my knees with his lady's behind, he leaned over her shoulder and taught me a lesson which I, along with most of the men of my generation, had forgotten.

"Give in, give in, give in," he urged in a powerful old man's voice greened by his pleasure. "Give in, give in, give in, give in," until the advice became lyrics and the lyrics became a way to break my bonds. His urging should have been enough to drag me to my feet and pull me into the anonymous, jangly, many-backed beast that the dancers had become. It was my moment to grow up. It was a free gift from an old man who had glanced across from his culture to mine and knew the watering I needed.

Alas, I was not ready and when I left, still no dancer, I could see, for just a passing moment, sadness for me in his ancient eyes. Then he was back to his swively lady and to the music which had oiled him.

Years later, in a smoky cellar in old Soho in London, another woman, impatient with my refusal to dance with her, pulled me onto the tiny dance floor. This time the

music was disco and over the din she ordered, "Dance !"
I still could not. Then softer, almost pleading, she murmured, "Give in."

The words snapped at me like a hypnotist's fingers
and I felt my hips unlatch and I danced. I had heard
again the old man urging, "Give in." It is a lesson that
too many of us never learn, a lesson all women are born
knowing. In that cellar in Soho I learned first to give
in to the music and later with enormous gratitude, to
give in to my life and most important of all, to give in to
the sea.

I learned to dance, but almost too late. For from the
dance floor to a tiller of a sailboat bounding about in a
wild sea is a very small distance indeed.

A TALE OF A MARK AND TWO BILLS

At the age of fifty, when most men are dickering for ceme-
tery plots, Bill decided to sail solo around the world *via
the great Southern capes*. At fifty-two, having inveigled
rich men to help him, he departed from Philadelphia
where we had helped prepare his untried boat for an ultimate passage.

Sailors have done this before but no one has ever approached this daunting program with Bill's particular
package of unknowns. Any sailor with no ocean experience and no income from family or elsewhere would give
serious pause to undertaking a solo circumnavigation.
Being black, Jewish, and poor might not be considered
detriments but when you think of the state of the world
today they surely are not advantages. Unless you are Bill
Pinkney.

Bill Pinkney, born in the south, seamy side of
Chicago, educated only to high school, clawed his way out

of two ghettos to become a successful yuppish marketing type. Black Bill had not only to be the best marketer in Revlon, the best Jew in his congregation, the best sailor on the Great Lakes racing circuit, he had also to be the best black in the local NAACP.

In retrospect, considering the divergent pressures and demands that such a life program put on Bill's baldy, grizzled head, all of these confrontations might not be such a bad preparation for taking a 47-foot sailboat alone around Cape Horn. Rubbing elbows beyond his birth, Bill took to sailing on the Great Lakes with the verve that only a poor, black, Jew could muster. Plunked down amidst a white business community, he had to exceed Caesar's wife in purity and excellence.

At the very least the prospect of getting out alone and putting all of his emotional, intellectual, and racial baggage behind him must have seemed to Bill to be a kind of heaven and not the hell that a solo circumnavigation evokes in most sailors' minds.

Peter Vanadia, who ran a true sailor's yard along the river in Philadelphia, called me one afternoon. He heard I was back from sailing and insisted that I meet a sailor who had just arrived to ready his boat. The next Saturday my son called to tell me that I must come down to the yard. This, said my son, was my kind of guy. When two sailors whom I respect tell me to do something I do it.

The boat was up on a trailer just in from the overland trip from Chicago. She had been violently introduced to a bridge abutment which had torn out some starboard lifelines, bent the steering pedestal, and committed sundry other indignities which an old lady in a hurry with a horrendous passage ahead of her really did not need. Her name was COMMITMENT, changed from LONESTAR, the boat in which Mark Schrader had made his own solo cir-

cumnavigation. Bill had acquired her from Mark, a tale of
its own.

There was no question in Bill's mind that he was now
going to do it. The long voyage of finance and preparation, of wheedling and coaxing, and the battle with self
when time after time he lost heart, was over. Bill Pinkney
stood by COMMITMENT, a little lost. His dream, crouched
on a trailer waiting to be tamed, was jelling, very, very
real, in front of him. Like dreams and wishes, the moment
comes when your best-worst fears are realized. The arrival
of COMMITMENT at the shore of the Delaware, in smelling
distance of the open sea, reminded Bill of the wild sea
ahead of him. Momentary indecision was suppressed. Bill
was ready.

Bill opted that his passage would make a statement
for those black kids who, for lack of patterning, would
spin out their time in poverty and drugs in the ghettos of
Chicago.

Bill had been that rare animal, a breed just emerging
in America, a black Yuppie. Having made the team and
joined the club, the thrill of achievement dribbled out and
a haunt of questions troubled him. Was the success game
worth the candle? Was the rest of his life to be a replay, a
dull *déjà vu*, of the time till now? Bill said no, and cast
about for a challenge with meaning, for the sensitive energy that bounced from pole to pole inside his head. Bill
would do what no other black had done before him. He
would sail, solo, around the world. And give to the sub
culture from which he had sprung a genuine, reproduce-
able hero.

And now commenced a series of events both bizarre
and unplannable. The Good Lord, obviously intent on
testing Bill on the wild Capes, had in store for Bill dra-
matic twistings that even Hollywood might reject.

When Bill came out of high school with no money for
college, he joined the Navy and served his time, eight
years, as a pharmacist's mate, alongside Bill Cosby. They

kept sometimes in touch over the years and when both Bills turned fiftyish, Pinkney confided to Cosby his dream. He asked Cosby for no assistance. Cosby passed the wild plan along to Armand Hammer.

The plan had now transmogrified more into a desire to raise the spirits of dispirited black kids than the sailing itself. The passage, the enormous solo effort, fell into the background as first Cosby, Hammer, and then others twanged to Pinkney's plucking. Without the commitment to the kids Cosby would not have listened, Hammer would never have taken the bait and, eventually, Bill would not have been able to get Schrader's great Valiant. The common thread was the kids.

There lies deep in the hearts of those who can do a stream of pity and guilt for those who cannot. Cosby, Hammer, Schrader and finally three, totally poles apart, folk from Boston succumbed to Bill Pinkney and succumbed to the kids.

Bill conspired with Margaret Harrigan of the Chicago school system and came up with a computer/satellite program which will allow the kids from Southside to follow, daily, Pinkney's progress. The computer connection branches and twigs out into all sorts of information relative to the precise spot on the globe in which COMMITMENT happens to be sailing. The kids are to be charged up with the adventures of Bill and the implied argument that they too can do it.

A very difficult program to resist and luckily many failed to resist. Half a million dollars worth of resistance went down the drain as three proper Bostonians, who told me they prefer to remain nameless (a true charitable act), shelled out three of the five of the green and gave Bill the opportunity to put himself seriously in harm's way.

COMMITMENT arrived in Philadelphia without paint, without supplies, without steering, and without a lot of other stuff with only a week to go.

Mark Schrader really made all possible when he allowed Bill to have his Valiant for the three-and-a-half years that it took to raise the money to buy it. Mark says he extended Bill's option to purchase 'two hundred times' and finally the money appeared. Schrader's interest, and his patience, goes back to Mark's own involvement in a school for handicapped kids. He knew what Bill's program could mean to the kids on the Southside, some more handicapped socially than his own kids had been handicapped physically.

Schrader also empathized with Bill over the agony of the major wheedle that Bill was going through. Telling the same tale of need over and over again was something that Schrader had himself been through and that, and the kids, caused Mark and his partners to wait years for money that might otherwise have come to them in months.

Bill's tale only tangentially touches on sailing. The reality of a solo will strike Bill only after all the unrealities of getting ready are behind him. In the week I spent with him in Philadelphia I watched calm patience crumble in the face of unnecessary emotional imposts. He began to yearn for the loneliness of the sea and suddenly the mystery of why solo sailors did it became clear.

Solo had, for Bill, become not a challenge, as it is usually described, but a salvation. Escape from the madding crowd is possible for only a lucky few who are eager to trade the impossibilities of dealing with the world for the impossibilities of the lonesome sea.

Solo, you are in harm's most extreme way, but solo you are truly free.

Can't you hear Bill's paean drift back down on the South Street Seaport from under the Verazzano, "Free at last, free at last, thank you Lord, we're free at last, thank God Almighty, we're free at last."

Postscript: Bill Pinkney survived his circumnavigation, taught a generation of black kids in Chicago that nothing is impossible and has been for years now pushing a big sailboat around the oceans teaching yet another generation of black kids that being black, Jewish, poor, and now old, are merely low barriers over which the dedicated, the committed may leap.

PETER OF GREENPEACE

Captain Peter said, "I cling to honesty." He said it as if he were not sure that he could and to Captain Peter honesty is all. We were sitting in his tiny cabin aboard RED SEA TRADER of which Peter was the skipper. He had been formerly the skipper of RAINBOW WARRIOR and the change from warrior to trader seemed to signal a passage in life to Peter. He was puzzled, and not a little depressed, over his separation from the good fight on Greenpeace. He was not at all sure just why he was pushing a clownish little container tramp around the dingier ports of hopeless East Africa rather than standing in a little rubber boat between whales and whalers' harpoons, charged with adrenalin and the absolute conviction that he was doing something good.

RED SEA TRADER is a converted oil rig service boat well into her declining years, perhaps months. She does the same job as the ancient camel caravans that used to roam the Red Sea coasts from Somalia to Morocco. She meanders, a more watery word than roam, between Djibouti, Aden and Ethiopia, picking up a handful of containers in Djibouti and depositing them, like large square eggs, in poorer ports that cannot accommodate the big container vessels. The passages last two, maybe three days and are deadly dull. The crew, save for the former skipper of RAINBOW WARRIOR, are lusty drinkers and nice guys but little else.

Peter sits with me in his little cabin and worries at his

new condition like a baby worries at a new tooth. He is a young man, at least by my ken if not by his, tall, Lincolnish and troubled.

"I cling to honesty," he repeats for perhaps the fourth time and expands it with, "that is why I am here and not back with Greenpeace."

His heart, he explains, is there but he can no longer be with them for, "while I agree with their aims I have come to suspect their motives." What he suspects are the media and the search for 'visuals' of Greenpeace. And his suspicion, entwined with his precarious clutch at 'honesty', drove him as far down from the modish excitements of the environmental battlements as he could get. Down, down into the ends of the world. Down into the lower reaches of the Red Sea where hardly anybody ever goes and where there are no whales to save, only starving people.

For occasional visitors he relived the glory days of Greenpeace. He told of the great battles in Iceland and the Antarctic, the councils of war wherein the Antichrist was confounded and brought to his knees. He spoke of the substitution of guts for guns and brains for the brute swoosh of the harpoon. He spoke of glee, exalting glee, over a pod rescued from the flenser's knives or of a single whale saved by a man in a rubber boat offering his own breast to the harpooner's gun. Peter had reached for, and found, the reason for his existence. He was at the front lines between the children of light and the children of darkness. His face, his whole being, was lighted by this knowledge.

And then the light darkened. He was back worrying again at the decision that had brought him to Djibouti and RED SEA TRADER. "I left Greenpeace because I began to doubt their motives, but do motives really count? Isn't it only what you do that matters? Could I not have," and here he twisted in the wind, "should I not have forgiven, overlooked their motives for the sake of the good I knew we were doing?" Peter had built himself a pair of horns from which his desperate grip on honesty would not let him dismount.

Peter was a second mate in the British Maritime Service, wandering through life and an insubstantial marriage, when, quite by accident he caught an early BBC documentary about Greenpeace. They put out a call for professional seamen and Peter thought, "Here is something I can do, something worth doing."

He quit his job, no great sacrifice as he tells it, and went down to Greenpeace where he was signed on as a volunteer (no pay, just bed and food). His first job was as second mate and then, shortly, he was made skipper of RAINBOW WARRIOR and for eighteen months he lived in the light until his conscience sent him to the darkness of Djibouti where I found him struggling with his own devil. After we spoke, he took RED SEA TRADER on a delivery to Aden. He was back in three days, deep in melancholy, unrousable.

Peter had received a call from Jane, his wife, who had just returned to England. She was pregnant. Peter's reaction was predictable and endearing. "Children? What will we leave for our children? What will their world be when we are through with it?" I left him to his misery but when I next saw Peter he was, as they say, up and about, his melancholy pushed into a secret place for some future consideration, replaced now by an irrepressible conviction that there was "something worth doing."

He had a new project. Jane had discovered a new Greenpeace. They were to stand not between whales and harpoons but between the helpless, hopeless folk of East Africa and poverty, disease, and starvation. "We call it 'Devon Sail' and it's about building a sailing ship," and here his voice speeded into a rush of explanation as if I might not stay to listen, "We will take kids from England in trouble with the law and make sailors out of them and sail down the coasts of Sudan and Ethiopia and Somalia and set up artisan workshops and teach agriculture and water technology and carry native goods back to England to sell and use the money for other trips. We will be only the first seed of many sailing ships who will copy and imitate us until we have a nation of little boats curing the desperate emptiness of our own young and filling the bellies of East Africa."

He barely paused to breath and added, "Write about it. We will need money and volunteers and boats and supplies and ideas. Reach out for us. Tell them what we are doing. Tell them of the help we need."

In the midst of the rush of passionate explanation Peter halted as if with a screech. "But we will not be the servants of your media. We will not show you starving kids like we showed you bludgeoned seal pups. We will not be your clowns for an evening's entertainment. We will use you and you will love it."

Peter had climbed down from his horns and was on the road again. Djibouti was already behind him. A new world of something worth doing was ahead. I am absolutely sure that some poor folk in poor East Africa, not many but some, will die later rather than sooner.

Hooray for Captain Pete.

THE SAILOR WHO TALKS TO GOD

I have always liked South Africans. They lump in my mind with the cowboys of our own West, with the insouciant Australians, and with the always congenial New Zealanders. Frontiersmen all. Self-reliant, self-assured, tough and resilient. No identity crises among this breed. They know their worth, stick hard to their beliefs, and are closer to nature than the rest of us.

I ran into Bob Schaafsma at the marina in Tel Aviv. His boat, draped with wind generators and antennas, sported a high poop deck and a wooden, boomless mast. It flew an unfamiliar flag and when I asked one of my more irreverent Israeli friends about the strange flag and the stranger looking boat, his answer was, "Oh, that's Bob Schaafsma. He's from South Africa. He talks to God every day."

Wild horses could not have kept me away after an introduction like that and, as I came to know Bob Schaafsma and his little brood, my faith in South Africans, Aussies, New Zealanders, and John Wayne was reaffirmed.

Bob had been a boat builder in a little town called Vredenberg near Cape Town until two years earlier. He was successful, respected, was just starting a family with his wife Diane, and had a good future. But Bob was having some difficulty with God. Bob did indeed talk to Him every day as do many others, but in Bob's case, God talked back. It seems that God was not satisfied with the good life that Bob was living, and not at all satisfied with the lot of the Jews in South Africa. "Go to Israel," Bob was urged, "live among the Jews and find the 'burden' there that I lay upon you."

Doing his Christian God's bidding and accepting his 'burdens' was easy for Bob. He sold his businesses, built a strange 48 footer with a lovely underbody, packed his two small kids, Funny Face and Popeye, and his seasick wife, Diane, aboard and sailed for Israel.

When I met him he had been in Israel 'among the Jews' for two years. No small feat for even a non-Israeli Jew, let alone a non-Israeli Gentile. But Bob was doing His bidding and he took Israel and its confronts in good humor. Better than I did, I must admit. He settled in, put his kids in school in Tel Aviv where they quickly became fluent in Hebrew and settled back to wait for the promised 'burden' to appear.

In long conversations with God, Bob became aware that the task being urged upon him was no less than to

save the Jews of South Africa. Not only to save them but
to develop a means whereby South African Jews would
find it possible to emigrate back to Israel carrying, as
God (indeed a Jewish God) put it, "all their worldly
goods."

Bob's God and Bob believed that the only salvation
for the scattered Jews of the Diaspora (the world other
than Israel) was to ingather them into their own country.
Like many fundamentalist Christians, Bob believed that
the Second Coming could only happen in old Jerusalem
and when all the Jews of the world had gathered in what
God called 'Palestine'. Bob's part of this worldwide crusade was South Africa. His Christian God had informed
him that He had chosen others to ingather the Jews from
other nations.

But Bob's problem was complicated by the reluctance
of South Africa to lose its Jews and to lose the capital that
the emigrants would take with them. How to get them out
of South Africa safely, unobtrusively and "with all their
worldly goods," that was the burden.

The plan that Bob hit upon has the dizzying quality of
revelation. When I first heard his idea it sounded strange,
improbable, impossible. Then I sensed its wonderful au-
dace, its cold and direct logic. If the Jews of Germany had
had a Bob Schaafsma, who knows how many more might
have survived.

Bob's burden, which he accepted with pride and dignity, was to sail back to South Africa and design and build
a fleet of 50-foot sailboats, with beam enough to take cars
and house trailers and furniture and all the other worldly
goods of the Jews. Then, one by one, they would sail off
on a 'short' cruise, unbothered by customs or financial
folk and quietly disappear.

For the very, very rich the keels would, on dark and
secret nights, be poured of purest gold.

I came to accept Bob's vision, to want it to work no
matter how crazy it sounded or how many obstacles I

could see. It was a scheme, a crusade, that made Bob, successful or not, a bit larger than life, a bit more for history than for now. Vision, real vision, goofy or not, is a scarce commodity in our secular, workaday, lackaday world. Should someone with a wild idea and a wild eye come down your pike, count yourself lucky and boost the dreamer along. Who knows, he may be the one the world has been waiting for.

Bob preceded me down the Red Sea by a few weeks, he on his way to South Africa and me on my way toward the America's Cup races in Australia. I caught up with him just north of Port Sudan. It seemed he had been waiting for me. He had no SatNav as I did and he did not want to risk his little family among the treacherous reefs of that desperate sea. He said God had suggested that he sail along with me. I was enormously flattered.

We proceeded south. Off Ethiopia I was dismasted. I had to run for that inhospitable coast to jury rig. Knowing the monstrous difficulties that a South African boat could face in that black, Communist country, I called to Bob not to risk his family and to go along without me. His instant answer was a wave of his hand and a snort, "We started together and we will stick together."

As it turned out we did have bad problems on that terrible coast and had to run for it in the dark of a moonless night to escape boats full of armed Ethiopians hot after our hides. After our escape, safe in the Gulf of Aden, we met for farewells. He was off toward South Africa and I to Djibouti to step a new mast. As we said goodbye I took little Popeye on my knee and asked if he had not been a little scared during our escape from Ethiopia.

He turned to me and with eyes as open as only an eight year old's can be, he said. "Scared? No."

"How come," I asked. "I sure was scared."

" 'Cause," he said quietly, "Jesus wont let anything bad happen to me."

I glanced up and caught a wide and contented grin spreading across Bob's face.

I may not be a believer myself, but I believe in folk like Bob Schaafsma.

CHAPTER THREE

Curtain-raising People

ALL OF THE PEOPLE in this chapter have suffered under the oppression of a totalitarian regime and yet find their way to breath the air of freedom. The common thread is the emergence of the individual.

Mr. Ghou and Miss Dung pave the way for a capitalist economy in communist China. The Russian sailors racing against the Americans realize how arbitrary or nonsensical the rules of the Racing Committee are. Russitch and his family leave a Gorbachev-era Russia for freedom in the West.

MR. GHOU AND MISS DUNG

Long before the recent opening of China, I sailed my boat up the Yangtze, turned left at the Hwang Pu, and made a triumphant passage up that busy river that runs through the Bund in the heart of Shanghai.

Our boat was the first American, or, for all I know, first of any sailing boat to have made that voyage since World War II. We were feeling pretty good in a sneaky sort of way since we thought how clever of us to have conned the Chinese with a cock-and-bull story about wanting to build fiberglass yacht factories for them. All we really wanted was permission to sail into Shanghai. Who conned whom I am not sure, but when we left two years later we had indeed built the first yacht factories in China in a joint venture with the Chinese. The venture is still pumping along although I cut and ran as soon as it showed any promise of making money. I have this kind of economic death wish.

But this is not about business entanglements with Marxist China. I write here about two lovely people, Mister Ghou and Miss Dung, who, with even less experience than we had, guided us safely between capitalist Scylla and communist Charybdis.

Mister Ghou and Miss Dung were, ostensibly, our translators in the great yacht building enterprise. She had a little English and he had considerably less. In discussions with our opposites at the Shanghai Shipbuilding Corporation I would speak to Miss Dung, Miss Dung would pass it along to Mister Ghou, who would then reformulate the message in terms acceptable to his superiors who had no English at all. God knows what came out of the other end of the pipeline but everyone was good natured, pragmatic and dedicated, so great precision did not matter. Indeed, in China, great precision rarely matters in personal relationships. It is feeling rather than precision that rules.

We all became great friends and some worthwhile projects were undertaken. We can at least claim the first western-designed luxury fiberglass vessel ever built in China. It was designed by Bob Perry and called Periwinkle. It was a beautiful dinghy of some nine feet.

Mister Ghou, Miss Dung, and their leadership in the Shanghai Shipbuilding Corporation had just received from above startling, almost 'counter-revolutionary', instructions to do business with the West. At that moment, except for Nike, we were the only westerners in Shanghai and we knew damnall about the problems we were facing. We had brought with us all of the traditional capitalistic impedimenta. We were not going to change. It would have to be they who would have to learn our new ways and accommodate to the times.

Without a hint of theoretical background the corporation was entering into the morass of international free competition. It was like unfreezing an ice age man, taking away his campfire, and handing him a microwave. It was impossible.

But it was done. And from the patterns that developed, Chinese leaders at all levels began to learn about the West.

But at the point, at the cutting edge, were Mister Ghou and Miss Dung. Since their superiors, trying to respond to some scary, shifty hints from Beijing, knew not even what questions to ask, Ghou and Dung became the real entepreneurs, among the first who set in motion the learning process which has now brought China to the possibility of interface with the West.

In fact, in blind anticipation of events of which we could not even dream, we called our brave new company the China Interface Corporation. While the Chinese leadership had long and effective familiarity reaching (interfacing with?) their own people, they had not the slightest notion of how tender are the strands needed to cross connect two wildly differing intellectual, cultural, and economic sets.

This became the job of these two young people who were to have acted only in the capacity of translators. In the event, when they translated into Chinese our needs and desires, the results were as incomprehensible to their leadership as if the words had been left in English.

Let me give two instances. One of the shipyards, which we would have to supervise, was located two hours outside of Shanghai by way of overcrowded and unsatisfactory public transportation. In order to make the western supervisor's job possible, we first asked for a car and driver. This was refused out of hand. No one, not even the highest official of their corporation had such luxury. But we had softened them up, and when next we asked, as an alternative to a car, for a small apartment to be built within the factory space to allow our supervisor to live in during the week, they took it under consideration.

It became Ghou and Dung's job to explain the unnatural concept of privacy. They had to shape our needs in their own minds first and then make the wrenching shift to our 'side' so that they might argue the need for even so slight a privilege. The living space was finally built. We undertook to furnish it, refrigerator and all, but when I left two years later the acceptance process had not progressed far enough to allow us to move in. Our supervisor was still commuting.

It is characteristic of Chinese leadership that when an event or a process is not fully played through, they are willing to allow it to progress to incompletion. A most aggravating condition and one which Ghou and Dung had most difficulty conveying. The simple idea that we were more interested in completed events than in learning from a process (we, after all, had already learned) was more than they were able to convey to their chairman. The 'private living space' became an undergraduate learning arena for the next—the now—generation of their economic leaders. But it was due to the ability of Ghou and Dung to see that any interfacing at all took place.

Another event took even our translators, now firmly committed to us, by surprise. We noticed that the workmen assigned to us would nod off at about three in the afternoon. They had been on the job since eight and still had three hours to go. By our capitalist sensibilities we objected to paying for three hours of labor that we never received. When we asked Ghou and Dung what they thought the problem was, they, with more sophistication than we had given them credit for, suggested that it was the result of diet. Our Chinese workmen were living on an assigned intake of only 1500 calories a day. With so little energy available, sleep was the obvious answer.

We had identified a problem, asked a question, received a cogent answer. We had all of our capitalist ducks lined up in a row. The solution was obvious. We would provide, at our expense, a three o'clock tea break, with plenty of sugar, and sweet cookies. The food would cost us the equivalent of about ten minutes of a workman's time. A simple matter of maximization of profit.

When Ghou and Dung were asked to convey our suggestion they were aghast. Providing extra reward, especially of food, for merely doing one's duty was unheard of. All must be treated equally. They reminded us that they themselves had never even been allowed to sit down to lunch with us. They had to eat separately with their comrades. It was an impossible request which, when pressed, was summarily turned down.

But the seed was planted, Ghou and Dung lost that battle but, from the longer view of what is happening in China today, a war was being won.

And now for the best part. In a nation in turmoil, as postwar China has been since its birth, the emergence of an individual is an unlikely event. Amid the stark and equal billions of China, amid the chancy shifts and lurchings of revolutionary polity, a strong spirit may indeed be thrust to the top only, alas, too often to drown in the tumultuous froth of change.

In this case, all odds against, the tossed coin stood on edge. A friend just back from Shanghai called with regards from Mister Ghou. It seems that he has set himself up as a private consultant to foreign firms wishing to do business in China: office, secretary, typewriter, suit, shirt, tie and . . . Miss Dung.

Go get 'em, Ghou and Dung.

SHANGHAI ADVENTURE

The Shanghai Department Store No.1 is a large, five-story building in central Shanghai. Each of the five floors is crammed with nondescript goods, of value only to the Chinese peasants who shop there. When the country people were allowed to visit the big city—permission had to be requested and was rarely granted—No.1 (as it shall be known hereafter) was where they went, like a Long Island world class shopper homing in on Madison Avenue. No.1 was always crowded with comrades who had about a dollar a month of disposable income to lavish on goods of high luxury such as soap and toothbrushes. A good deal of thought and consideration goes into that expenditure in China and most of the decisions were taken at No.1. In all of China there was no larger array of consumer goods than at No 1, where you almost always had a selection of one from which to choose.

But this tale is not about consumer goods and department stores, it is about a very brave Shanghai lady who had established her turf and laid her snares in No.1. She was there because it was only at No.1 that the opportunity for her to meet a western male existed. It was the only time that any sort of erotic adventure occurred to me in all the many months I spent in that sexually antediluvian country. This tale is really about the desexualization of China by its revolution and is best told through my adventure with this bravest and most pitiful of women in that crowded land.

There were no bars or night clubs or dance halls or cafes or any sort of dens of assignation in the entire country. There was simply no traditional meeting ground where a Chinese lady of the evening could interact with a foreigner. As a result, No.1 had become the swinging singles' club of Shanghai. If you were looking for a little action, it was always to be found in the fabric department on the third floor. It seems that Chinese ladies with the itch get turned on by the availability of large bolts of cloth.

It was not only that meeting places did not exist, it was also that any traffic with us barbarians from the West was considered politically deviant and culturally *de trop*. Even the people with whom one might have legitimate business relationships (such as I had) were not allowed to mix even for an innocent cup of tea, let alone for the delightful dalliance of the mixing of genes.

The accepting of gifts of any kind was prohibited and dangerous to the giftee. Under its quaint system of old fashioned Marxism, tipping, or the payment for any personal services outside the system, was treasonable. This made it difficult but, as we shall see, not impossible for an entrepreneurially inclined lady intent on going into business for herself. Marxist China had been successful in exorcising most of its history and culture, but the ancient and honorable profession of concubinage was ineradicably graven into the memory of the more ambitious and more beautiful ladies of Shanghai. But it all became very difficult.

What made it more difficult was that the lady spoke not a word of my language and I had not a word of hers, but in some transactions spoken language is only an impediment anyway. The deed got done, or almost done, in the marvelous use of eyes and body language. Without speech to disenchant, it was the most erotic sexual confrontation imaginable. I have mused since on the women whom I have turned off by a thoughtless word and those women who froze me with an inelegant phrase. Except for poets, wooing should be accomplished by sighs and sibilants. It is by far the most effective mode.

The lady, in her terror of discovery, was a mistress of that quiet art. Where everything had to be suggested, as in the highly policed No.1, everything was fantasy. Where everything was forbidden, even the curl of an eyebrow was maddening and the slight, seeming accidental touch of a hand retaught the excitements of puberty.

She was dressed just slightly outside of her milieu. Not flashily, in the *demi-monde* tradition of the West, but just a bit out of synch with the shapeless bodies about her. She wore boots with small sharp heels and a tailored tartan skirt which any self-respecting western whore would not be seen in at a dog show but which, in that drab setting, was a piece of black Victorian erotica.

She wore a high collared silk Chinese shirt and while she was not sexy in our sense, she was certainly interesting. She was slim and had a pleasant face which, during all the hours I knew her, wore the look of a basset hound. A very pretty basset hound but a very worried one.

And she had plenty to worry about. If she were picked up at her trade she would, at best, be banished to hard labor as a farmer on a distant commune. She was taking her life in her hands in exchange for what?

As I made my purchases she took them from the clerk without a word, as if she had been assigned by the tourist agency to be my guide on a shopping spree. When we walked out of No.1 she insisted, silently, on carrying everything and it was in that manner that we made our way up to my hotel room. Unfortunately, the disguise was less than perfect, she being too pretty, and she attracted curious looks from the hotel staff.

In our room we commenced, she shyly, the usual *pas de deux* that precedes sex whether it be paid or unpaid. However long before things became interesting there commenced a stream of hotel staff incursions which were designed, I am sure, to prevent any unmarxist cohabitation. It was clear that we had to get out.

We went for a walk, in search of someplace to do the deed, or in any event a place for a little heavy petting, but in Shanghai there simply is no privacy. We tried the park where she managed to insinuate my hand onto her wee little breast but that was as far as we got when they closed the park on us.

I was ready to give up, but my little Chinese lady was adamant and we started walking into darkening Shanghai as the sun set. We had walked for miles with hardly a word when she pulled me into a dim hallway and signaled that I was to wait for her. She would go upstairs to arrange, she sighed, for a place for us.

I waited in the gloom for an hour while everyone in the building, alerted to my presence, came to check me out. I stayed not only because I wanted the lady but, if the truth be known, I was lost with not the vaguest idea of how to get home and no one to ask. Taxis did not exist and I had no way to know where any of the few buses that passed were headed.

It became evident that the people in the flat upstairs, to which she had wanted to take me, were spooked. So much so that she herself never did come back down. I found my weary way home that night by reasoning that since my hotel was near the river, I must go down hill to reach it. It took me four hours, four unsatiated hours, to make it.

Before we had left my hotel, before it became clear that we could not consummate there, I tried to give her money. She refused. I had a treasure of western clothing in my luggage which she also refused.

"Well, what do you want?" I silently signaled.

"Perhaps," she charaded, "a piece or two of hotel soap?"

I nearly cried.

All she had ever wanted from me was a fleeting touch of the West. She was risking her freedom, and throwing in her body, in exchange for a moment of contact with someone, anyone, from outside the dead life that she sensed she was living.

NICHITA AND SOME OTHER QUEER FISH

I found no big game fish hungering after my hook in the Black Sea. But I found two things, both larger than life, that made the journey more than worthwhile. I met Nichita. And I happened upon two clever fish that, while only feet rather than yards in length, might just be worth a week or so of a dedicated angler's time.

I was introduced to the two remarkable fish by Nichita Ion, who was my mentor and guide in Mamaia, Romania. He is a huge man who towers two handspans over run-of-the-mill Romanians. His face only comes to life when he talks about fish. At other times speaking seems a chore with silence and contemplation to be preferred. But when he speaks of fish this large, no-nonsense man becomes poetic. He sees fish as worthy foes in the ageless engagement between man and fish. When he describes men who have succeeded in snaring the remarkable grey mullet of the Black Sea, his voice rises in adulation. These men are the stuff of heroes. They had bested the best. They were Priam at Troy and, indeed, as Nichita tells it, to inveigle the mullet something as subtle as a wooden horse is needed.

"No," he assures me, dashing my hopes, "there are no big game fish in the Black Sea, but there are fish a tenth the size and ten times as clever. No ordinary man could be expected to take such fish as these."

Nichita is the guru of Black Sea fishing. Fish are his private passion. In a country where half the men claim fishing as their hobby, Nichita is Romania's Isaak Walton. One rainy afternoon along the deserted, wintry beaches of the Black Sea, he spoke of the two very special fish in his life. The first was the grey mullet and the second an animal dubbed, for good reason, the sea killer.

"The Grey Mullet is the smartest fish in the world. It must be approached with knowledge, caution and respect. Even before setting out for a catch you must first locate the only bait that the Mullet," Nichita capitalized out of respect, "will take. It is a single species of sea worm that lives only among the dead white shells buried in the sand on very limited areas of the sea bottom. If you do not know where to find the worm, and few do, you will never catch the fish. The Mullet will rise to no other bait."

Even for the mullet the worm is an elusive creature. It sticks its mouth from the shells and sand only a few millimeters to draw in the passing waters for plankton. The worm presents a tiny target and the hungry mullet wants more than only the worm's head. It is the mullet's 'nature', as Nichita calls it, to bite deep into the sand with speed and violence, so as to get as much of the worm as possible in one bite.

This flashing speed of attack presents the first problem to the fisherman. Since the hit on a worm-baited hook is so furious, the fish, whose mouth is tender and soft, is likely to lose the hook in the violent moment of taking it.

Should the hook hold the fisherman sets himself for battle but the mullet appears to have disappeared. In fact, with a speed that far outruns the angler's ability to take in line, he sets a beeline toward the angler. When the befuddled fisherman suspects he has lost his fish and lets the line go slack, the mullet flashes into the air in breathtaking leaps of three and four feet above the surface of the sea and snaps its body to shake loose the hook.

"The Mullet is purposely," so says Nichita, and who am I to contradict, "using the lead weight on the line in the water to drag the hook from its mouth." A bit too much lead will tear the hook from the mullet's tender mouth. A bit too little weight and the motion of the hook will not satisfy the mullet. Since the mullets vary widely in weight it is only a matter of luck that the perfect match occurs between fish and sinker weight.

After the leaps the mullet rockets around the line in a further attempt to free itself. The sharp and swift turns, so fast they cannot be followed by the fisherman, usually create enough of a drag to free the hook. As if all this were not enough, the fish must not be allowed to get into shallow water where the friction of its body along the bottom is also enough to tear the hook from its mouth. Nichita says this fishy ploy is intentional.

At the side of the boat the mullet is too fast to net and too likely to lose the hook from its mouth in any attempt by the fisherman to lift the fish by the line. Puzzled, I asked Nichita how in the world does any one ever catch such a resourceful fish. "Only by accident," was his mysterious reply.

"When we gather on cold nights around a fire and exchange tales of the great fishermen, the most respected are those who have taken this fish. A man who takes a Grey Mullet is marked for life. A man who takes a large Grey Mullet may well be talked about even after his death."

"Have you taken a mullet?" I asked.

Nichita looked down on me for a moment from his six feet seven and said, quietly and with a barely hidden flash of pride, "A few."

Even I know a guru when I meet one.

The sun was well down and the chill from the blowing in of the Black Sea burrowed through my jacket, fur hat and muffler. Nichita strode along by my side, bareheaded in a light windbreaker. He scarcely noticed the bluster. He was thinking about fish.

Without preamble, after a long and chilly hike, Nichita commenced the story of the other fish, the sea killer of the Black Sea.

"A Sea Killer finger," he began, "is a finger that has been chopped off at the first knuckle. Nine times out of ten the owner of such a finger is a fisherman and the missing part was given as ransom to a Sea Killer already landed. Once the fish is in your boat the most extreme caution must be exercised. If you take a small Sea Killer it is necessary to immobilize the fish firmly in your armpit as you remove the hook. In a large fish it is necessary to kneel with both knees on the fish to safely immobilize it.

"The teeth of the Sea Killer," Nichita continued, warming to his subject as I froze on the strand, "are like those of the shark. It has two rows of teeth, one behind the other and slightly offset. Like this," Nichita held his palms together with one set of fingers nestled between the other, "so that when it bites the two sets of teeth can grind off a finger or through another fish with great efficiency. Only the Sea Killer and the shark have developed such an awful bite. But that is the least interesting thing about this fish."

"And the most interesting?" I urged.

"The most interesting is that the Sea Killer will continue to kill and eat as long as there is prey about. It ravenously attacks and tears apart and attempts to eat without regard to hunger or, indeed, without regard to its ability to take in more food. With a belly jam packed full, it simply continues to kill and eat, all the while spitting back up that which it is unable to swallow. It is a debacle!" Nichita said using the French pronunciation. "A true frenzy of killing. The waters about are in turmoil with terrorized fish attempting to escape and the Sea Killer slashing at everything that moves. When there is no more prey the Sea Killer stops eating, but not until then."

Nichita fell silent for a few moments, contemplating this dreadful mistake of nature. "There is no explaining its actions. The killing does not help its survival. It is an antisocial fish. A hooligan fish," he added with passion.

But his distaste eased toward admiration as he described the bizarre trickery of the sea killer in escaping the angler's hook.

"It will not strike a line on a reel. The motion of a reeled hook is too smooth to simulate the motion of its panicked victims which twist and turn in furious motions of escape. Not even by jerking a long rod to and fro can the Sea Killer be enticed. The hook must be pulled through the water by hand. Like this," Nichita demonstrated as he threw first one hand against his chest and then the other simulating a quick and jerky drawing in of a hand-held line. He looked like Tarzan beating his breast with long and flailing arms.

"In this manner the lure is made to appear to be a fleeing dinner and the Sea Killer will not fail to strike at anything in which it has instilled horror. But while it will strike your bait and set the hook, its two rows of teeth simply crush the steel and it is free with half your hook still in him.

"But the real deviltry of the Sea Killer appears when the fish is unable to bite through the steel. The fish swims off at great speed, whirls about, and speeds directly toward the boat like a torpedo. It slams head first into the side of the boat in an effort to dislodge the hook. It looks like nothing less than a personal attack by the ferocious fish in an attempt to get at the fisherman and tear him apart. Although you may know in your mind that the fish is merely trying to free itself you feel in your heart that you are its target. It is very frightening.

"Most of the time, since the jaw is so hard, it will knock the hook out and be off to the relief of the poor fellow in the boat who, by now, is not at all certain that he wants this devil aboard.

"That is not all," Nichita added. "If the Sea Killer fails in all its attempts to free itself then it will swim under the boat and pull the line along the metal strip that protects the keel till the line parts. What a fish!"

Later I asked Nichita if the mullet and the sea killer were not the ultimate challenge for a fisherman and would

not my fishermen friends in America make the long journey to meet such tricky fish. He discouraged me.

"Alas," he actually said 'alas', "the fish are unpredictable. The Mullet rarely returns to the same place twice
and usually meanders along in underwater streams of un-
detectable differences which it likes best. The Sea Killer
can only be located when the sea birds are sighted rushing
to devour the results of his havoc. I could never guarantee
that a visitor would hook, let alone land, a Grey Mullet or
a Sea Killer."

Nichita was curiously unconvincing . . . as if he did
not want his precious fish to be descended upon by ignorant anglers from the West. Even if they did bring along
hard currency. Some matters, among even socialist fishermen, are sacred.

RACING THE RUSSIANS

It wasn't easy. The Russian crews could not have been
nicer. Sailors, after all, are sailors, but the officials, in
spite of gold-toothed smiles and protestations of cama-
raderie, were distressed by the Americans' showing on the
first day of the Black Sea regatta. This was the seventeenth year that the regatta had been held in the waters
off the city of Odessa. This was the first year that any but
communist boats had competed. This year the Russians
were faced with three hot U.S. teams, two from St Mary's
College, which takes its racing very seriously, and the
third a pick-up team of old Citadel sailing buddies from
Charleston and other cities of the Confederacy. Things
started out hot and rapidly got hotter. Ultimately both
sides came away with a deeper understanding of the problems and pluses of the other. But there were some very
tense moments when the thaw of *glasnost* lost out against
the cold war of suspicion.

In strange boats and strange waters, using all Soviet gear, three American crews came in one, two, three in the first of five heats. The Russian sailors against whom they were competing were excited and pleased at the results. The Russians, so long cut off from sailing in the West, watched and learned and, as sailors do the world over, gossiped and compared. As the Americans, one by one, overtook and passed them, the signs of approval and encouragement were matched with smiles of good sportsmanship.

But on the second race the referees of the Black Sea Cup and the officials of the Odessa Yacht Club so delayed the American crews at the start that any chance of winning, or even of a fair race, were left behind at the gun.

At the gun the three American crews were still held inside the club waters as immigration officials lazily checked passports while the Russian boats were half a mile away at the starting line. The Russians held that any foreign boat leaving port, even for a race within Odessa Bay, would have to be cleared out as if they were leaving Russian waters. Oleg, a nifty Russian sailor, pleaded that the race be delayed until the U.S. crews were released and in place. The chief referee agreed to wait. He then turned around and fired the starting gun while the U.S. boats were still at dockside in the grip of molasses-slow officials. Suspicions arose that the delay was intentionally arranged to give the Russian boats a leg up. It was a reasonable assessment considering the problems of language and differences in culture.

When the gun went off Oleg begged the director of the club at least to be allowed a motor boat to tow the U.S. yachts, already late, to the starting line. The answer was, "*Nyet!*" with no explanation.

It seemed to the Americans at the time that the Russian *apparat* had decided to win the race at all costs. If the Soviets were being unfair their tactics were as transparent as a bottle of Stolychniya and as effective as a bucket tied to the keel.

In another official move that was perceived by the Americans as detrimental, it was decreed that each U.S. boat (not the Bulgarian, the Romanian, or any other communist boats) would have to carry one Russian as crew. The American crews had sailed together since childhood and needed a non-English speaking supercargo about as badly as the U.S.S.R. needed more bureaucrats. The two St Mary's boats agreed. They argued that in spite of the difficulty of carrying a Russian sailor, they wanted to show their appreciation to the Russian sailors who were panting to sail with them.

Squeaky, the U.S. skipper of MAESTRO, was less inclined to be cooperative. An unintimidated southern boy from Charleston, Squeaky knew how to say no. He simply said, "*Nyet!*" and sailed off. Nobody raised a finger. The Russians are great at creating obstacles but lousy at enforcing them.

Oleg, who had been to the U.S. with his crew for the Block Island doings and who had come to love and respect American racers, nearly blew a glow plug. Last seen, after this 'race' was started, he was complaining loudly and demonstrating his distress by putting his hand under his tee shirt over his heart and pounding away. His Russian heart, he said, "was bursting with frustration and anger."

In a moment of peasant's revenge or of utter ineptness, take your pick, the goodwill and affection so carefully nurtured between sailors who held in common their love for racing was soured by what appeared to be a clear attempt to encumber the Americans. In this land of deep suspicions, paranoia is easy to come by. The efforts of the People-to-People Committee, who had brought the Americans here, the efforts of countless Russians, and the expenditure of scores of thousands of dollars were being wasted. We could all have stayed at home.

But class will out and there must be justice because
MAESTRO starting half an hour late came in first. The team
from Charleston had picked up its half hour handicap and
then some. Ultimately the win was taken away from MAE-
STRO and given to the Russian boat BRAVO that finished
half an hour behind MAESTRO. That means that the committee had to correct over an hour for BRAVO to win. No
mean feat.

ODYSSEY, one of the St Mary's boats, would have had
a chance in that race but the sails the Soviets had laid on
them were hopeless so ODYSSEY took to hunting for wind
where no one else did. Dangerous stuff, taking flyers like
that, but they had little option since MAESTRO and ARIZONA
were both faster boats.

It was MAESTRO that got the Soviet goat. In the third
race, a hundred miler, MAESTRO took an early lead and
was gone . . . shot out of a cannon. It was a clean start,
no shenanigans on the committee boat. But the committee boat had shot off the 10- and the 5-minute flares at
the same time. None of the Russian crews seemed upset
but it puzzled the hell out of the three U.S. crews. The
flare episode, an act without reason or logical explanation, caused suspicions that perhaps the problem was
not evil intent but pure ineptness on the part of the officials. Some Americans more inclined to doubt the charge
of unfairness were reduced to charging the committee
with lack of organization and experience if not down-
right stupidity.

The Americans were determined to keep not only a
sharp eye to weather in this race but an even sharper eye
on the committee. It was like the boxer who, after a bad
round, was told by his trainer that the "other guy didn't
lay a glove on you." The fighter then advised his trainer to
watch out for the referee, " 'cause somebody out there is
beatin' the bejesus outta me."

This time the Race Committee somehow succeeded in
giving MAESTRO, the major threat to the Russian boats, dif-

ferent instructions from all the others in the race. MAESTRO had been instructed to hold course for a 'three second light', in writing. The others were told to look for a committee boat stationed on an unlighted mark. MAESTRO, half an hour ahead of the pack, found the committee boat but no 'three second light' so they held on course in the pitch black night till their keel 'discovered' a spit of land across the bay to be known for all time as Teddy Turner Junior's Point. Having to make up twenty miles they still came in fourth out of a field of fifteen boats.

All the other boats, those with the good instructions, rounded the committee boat. It's damned hard to win a race with multiple instructions. MAESTRO again dropped out of first. MAESTRO, at this point, had been the first boat by far to 31 of the 34 marks in the race, and they were not winning.

It had become clear to most by now that the committee was simply so inexperienced and so disorganized that it could hardly find its stern with both hands. The suspicion of evil intent started seeping away. The Americans were no longer up in arms over 'unfairness'. Now they were embarrassed, as were their Russian hosts, at the depth of the confusion that reigned in the Race Committee.

The fourth race was thirty miles in broad daylight in sight of land. Under these circumstances the Americans figured that there was little that the committee could do to take away a win. The U.S. boats whipped across the starting line like it was a ski slope. MAESTRO, with the best sails and the most experienced crew, was gone with what little wind there was. It was 1, 2 and 3. It was getting boring. No matter what was thrown at them the U.S. boats' backsides became the marks, as long as they were still in sight, for the Russians.

What happened? The committee canceled the race. They had mistakenly laid out an extra mark. Embarrassment on both sides deepened and the Americans were about to be defeated not by fast boats but by fumbling referees.

By now the eighteen Americans on MAESTRO, ARIZONA and ODYSSEY had taken as much as sailorly flesh and blood could stand. What to do? Half said let's go home. The other half said let's beat their tails anyway. All agreed that winning would be no great honor and losing no great defeat. They were racing not against the Russian sailors, who to a man were as furious as the Americans were; they were racing against a Race Committee made up of incompetents. No matter how well the Americans sailed they were going to have the cup snatched away from them.

It was heartening to watch these young men (and one nifty young woman from St Mary's) gird up their loins and come back into the fray after repeated rebuffs and frustrations. They had raced four races, had won them all and had been finessed out of victory. Their cup was running away from them. There were still two races to go.

For this observer it is a genuine pleasure to report that by the fourth race the committee had finally gotten it all together. The last two races were as pure and as perfect as any in a western circuit and laid to rest the paranoia that had characterized the earlier races.

Ultimately MAESTRO won the regatta after having survived blows of ill fortune that would have sunk a less game crew. ODYSSEY survived the worst luck of all. In the fourth race, out of twenty four boats, only ODYSSEY rounded the correct marks. They should have had that race and might well have taken the cup but it was argued by the committee, with cogency, that they, the committee, were at fault in issuing instructions that only one boat out of twenty four understood. Bad luck for ODYSSEY but the admission of error by the committee further cleared the air. The last tendrils of the fogs of suspicion were drifting off.

In order to take the cup, MAESTRO felt that they needed firsts in the last two races and that is what happened. They were not easy races, not easy between the Americans and not easy against the Russians. They were hard fought battles in light air and the Russians just missed, not by much, cutting the mustard. They will be formidable opponents in the future.

The most heartening aspect of the regatta was the good sportsmanship demonstrated by both sides. Even before it became clear that the committee had more thumbs than the usual issue, the Americans pushed back their anger and concentrated on winning the races, yard by yard, mile by mile, breath of air by breath of air.

The best sailing team won. All agreed of that. But the real winners were peace and friendship. We came to understand that Russians do not have tails and they that Americans do not have horns. A small victory on the larger scene of world events but one which will echo long and loud around the streets of Charleston and in the cloistered halls of St Mary's College.

THE RABBI AND THE TORAH

In the course of our circumnavigation, we often sought out seas that were not regularly visited by cruising sailors. My own family was from the Ukraine. Since I am a history buff and had recently reread Apollonius tale of the passage of the sailing ship Argo in the Black Sea in search of the Golden Fleece, I was compelled to follow Jason's wake.

Sailing in the Black Sea is awkward. There are no weather reports, the sea is shallow, and the winds come from every which way. The shallow sea and the winds make for most unpleasant motions and I recall that once, in a passage from Istanbul to Odessa, we had aboard a

very unhappy passenger. The passenger was the Lady
Saline who had come along to do a piece on the travels
of UNLIKELY. She forever will remain in my mind's eye
when, after a day of the most abusive beating from winds
and seas, she announced with dignity: "Well, I guess it is
time to throw up now." And it was indeed time to throw
up. The passage was so bad and the seas and winds so
contrary, that it was one of the few times in fifteen years
that we turned and ran back, saving our bellies for a better day.

The liveliness and unpredictability of the Black Sea at
its surface belies the utter absence of life of the sea itself.
The Black Sea has a dead, black bottom from which its
name is derived. It is not an attractive place to be.

We came into the Soviet Union from the Black Sea in
1988 and landed in Odessa. 1988 was the year that Gorbachev saved the world from nuclear Armageddon and, in
the process, destroyed a great power. The U.S.S.R. went
down and with it the self-confidence and pride of the
Russian people, a very dangerous condition much like that
of Germany before World War II.

But in 1988, that was all in the future. In June of that
year UNLIKELY became the first western sailing vessel ever
to visit the port of Odessa. That port had been closed to
all western sailors since the 1917 revolution and since
cruising under sail, as we know it, only came of age in our
lifetime, the entrance of UNLIKELY was, for Odessa, an his-
toric event.

Curiously, there had been and still was a yacht club
founded by the minions of the tsar. The Odessa Yacht
Club was over a hundred years old in 1988 and had been
taken over by Soviet sailing clubs as a base for their own
limited efforts at racing small boats.

Cruising was out of the question. Even the departure
of a small fleet of 20 footers for a two-hour race had to be
arranged weeks in advance and the equivalent of an exit
visa had to be obtained.

Therefore, when a large—enormous in their eyes—private yacht appeared *sans* visa, *sans* commissars and *sans* permits, the event became a source of wonder for Russian sailors and a source of confused agony for the immigration people and the NKVD which was the Soviet Union's equivalent of the CIA.

A few months earlier, before Gorbachev's leap into history, we would have been at risk of a Soviet trial and jail and the loss of our vessel. But now all was confusion and transition. The past did not work anymore and the future was unknowable. The erosion of bureaucratic self-confidence had begun. No one knew what to do with us.

So the process of appeal to higher authority began. A process brought to a high art by *apparatchiks* terrified of making a mistake. First the mayor of Odessa, then the regional governor, then the Ukrainian authorities, and finally the NKVD leadership in Moscow were appealed to. Even the NKVD had no formula—very important in a Communist society—for a private yacht arriving without permission.

Ultimately the matter went to Gorbachev who telegraphed the mayor of Odessa with an approximate message over his own signature. Here was an absolute classic case of bucking down.

"In the matter of the vessel UNLIKELY, I have just declared all power to the local Soviets. So you guys make the decision."

Turmoil and dismay roiled about in the local government but since throwing us out would have been a larger, more abusive, decision than passively allowing us to stay, UNLIKELY became a footnote to history.

But the old habits of control and suspicion persisted and that persistence is the basis for the adventure of the spirit that followed.

Whenever UNLIKELY enters a port anywhere east of Suez or east of the Bosphorus I make it clearly known that

I am a Jew. This is a ploy that, for two reasons, confuses my hosts and grants a strange kind of protection to my boat.

In the first place, folk in those climes are all more or less wary of Jews and are accustomed to their own Jews hiding their identity. To proudly and unashamedly claim Jewishness disconcerted them to the extreme.

The second reason is more curious. The best known spy organization in the world is the Mossad, the efficient and dangerous counter-intelligence arm of Israel. It is better known in the East, better even than their own spies.

Evidently by simply announcing our Jewishness, the image of the feared Mossad was evoked, for why else would this strange vessel appear on their shores. Thus our hosts became even more wary.

I have been viewed as a Mossad agent in every arcane and esoteric port into which I ever sailed simply on the basis of telling folk I am Jewish. A real spy would certainly attempt to hide that fact. This never seemed to occur to my hosts. Furthermore it did not hurt that 40% of the population of Odessa were closet Jews.

At any rate, since I had caught the attention of Gorby himself and out of NKVD fears that I may be Mossad, I and my crew and UNLIKELY herself luxuriated under a blanket of warm and fuzzy protection.

We could do nothing wrong. In fact, the mayor of Odessa, unsolicited, had issued to me a document, which I still have, addressed to the police which declared that I had his permission to do anything I liked in Odessa except drive a car the wrong way up a one-way street.

And thereby hangs a tale.

The Jewish community, both those in a closet and the few who were out, was abuzz with this strange American who was not ashamed of his Jewishness. We were besieged with folk who, out of the side of their mouths, admitted to their real names which had long since been Sovietized for protection. They all seeked help and advice about how they should face the new dangers of transition now that the old dangers of Stalinism were abating.

We helped where we could, encouraged where we could not help, and, since the closed doors of the Soviet Union had cracked open a bit, we advised emigration.

By virtue of arriving on our own bottom, and being that rarest of beasts, a Jew who announced it, we were a major curiosity. I was soon summoned to meet the Chief, and only, Rabbi in Odessa. I was instructed to come alone.

The rabbi hemmed and hawed, took me upstairs to his study in the one synagogue in Odessa, locked the doors, pulled the blinds and announced that he was putting his life in my hands. I was not given the choice of either accepting or rejecting this heavy responsibility.

He did not quickly reveal why, but it was clear that he was terrified and had only brought himself to speak to me out of the strange circumstances that surrounded the visit of UNLIKELY.

After small talk and additional exhortations to secrecy, he revealed his terrible secret.

He had a Torah, a scroll of the law, the most holy instrument of Judaism, hidden away. It had been passed from rabbi to rabbi in secret in the half century since ownership of the scroll, the mere ownership of which represented a real danger. Had it been made known to the Soviet authorities, it would have been confiscated not as a religious icon but as a valuable work of art, all of which were, naturally, owned by the State.

"Why," I inquired, "tell me all this?"

The rabbi answered in Talmudic measures.

"Consider who you are, where you are. You are an announced Jew, an American under protection of your flag. You have been publicly acknowledged by Gorbachev himself and by virtue of all this, you have frightened the

NKVD into inactivity. More to the point, you own your own vessel and have the astounding freedom to come and go as you please."

I could not see where all this was leading. The rabbi continued:

"The odds, my friend, against a Jew arriving in a private sailing vessel in Soviet Odessa, protected against the NKVD and acknowledged by Gorbachev, must be truly astronomical odds. It is an event which could not happen for the past fifty years and now, at this moment, it has happened, here and now, to me. It is a gift from God."

I agreed that the odds were great and the rabbi finally revealed how these odds could become a blessing and why a gift from God.

"I have secreted away a Torah. It is the only thing of real value that I have in this world. I wish to emigrate to America but cannot do so without funds."

A light began to dawn. The rabbi continued.

"The Torah is held captive in the U.S.S.R. There is no way that it can be taken out of the country by sea or land or air except . . ."

I picked up the thought, "except by a Jewish sailor who just happens to be in Odessa and who can easily smuggle it out on his own boat."

The rabbi beamed with delight and we settled down to talk a little treason.

The deed was done. I wrapped the Torah in an old newspaper, like fish for the Sabbath, and tucked it under my arm. I sashayed past the armed guards thrown around UNLIKELY by the NKVD. I had long since corrupted them with U.S. cigarettes. I buried the precious package, now carefully waterproofed, in my bilge and sailed out of the crumbling Soviet Union to the blessed freedom of the West feeling like the finder of the Lost Ark. Eventually, through the sale of the precious Torah, I arranged that the penniless rabbi from Odessa would have $10,000 to start a new life awaiting him on his arrival in New York.

It is one of the few acts in my life about which I am inordinately, but undeservedly, proud. By no effort of my own I was able to serve the rabbi, serve my religion, serve my own country and, finally, serve, in my own small way, the cause of freedom.

The Universe cast the dice that day for the rabbi from Odessa, for Jews, for the sacred scroll, and for me the un-witting messenger.

For once, we all came up winners.

RUSSITCH

We came upon Ivan Russitch as the full import of a dying and repressive empire changed his life.

In 1988, as Gorbachev offered the first taste of free-dom to generations of Russians, we were the first private sailboat to pull into the port of Odessa since the Russian Revolution in 1917. Our passage around the world in UN-LIKELY had taken a jog to the north, through the storied Dardanelles and the narrow Bosphorus and, thus, into the Black Sea where we turned left and sailed toward the So-viet Union.

It was, for us, a moment of high exhilaration to watch a mighty nation and a passionate people move out of the darkness into the light.

It was, for the Russians, a moment of disbelief and de-light that freedom should happen in their lives. It was for the Russians, as we have come to realize, the discovery that the obverse of the offer of freedom was the pure, stark terror of the unknown.

We all run away from freedom in our own ways. We seek out limits and parameters within which we may more

comfortably move. We draw lines around our experiences
and say, with the ancient Portuguese navigators, "Beyond
here there be dragons." The lines we draw allow us a limited and acceptable freedom. Pure freedom, without limit,
paralyzes.

For Ivan Russitch the merest whiff of that purest of
oxygen was as if the old world had ended and a new world
was abirthing. The new world, for Ivan, held the reverse of
the repressions and the limitations of his life as a citizen of
Odessa. The iron grip of the secret police was weakening.
Incursions from the West, such as the arrival of UNLIKELY
at the 100-year-old Odessa Yacht Club, hastened that
demise.

The club had been formed in 1888 as a playground
for royalty and had somehow transmogrified itself into a
communist parody of its own history. Local sailboats
were few and ancient, the amenities of the club were
mean or mostly absent. But it was on the sea and Russian sailors still did come down to the sea to their sailing
ships.

Even in 1988 it was not a simple matter to hop
aboard and go asailing. Permission had to be obtained
days in advance. Only the most loyal Party members
held the narrow right to sail away from Odessa for fear
that sailors less committed sail on out to freedom. The
old habits of restraint and control perseverated even as
the very fabric of the Great Socialist Experiment was
shredding.

Those who met the standard of absolute loyalty
could go sailing. They found themselves, for some few
wild moments, in total charge of their own destinies. The
mastery of their own vessels and their own lives gave
them a taste of the freedom that all sailors experience as
they leave behind the constricting tentacles of even a free
society.

Ivan Russitch was not one of the blessed one but he
did fare much better than most. He had a car and, as the

head of the repair service for all auto transport in Odessa, he lived well. He had a lovely bit of land with a more than acceptable *dacha* in which he and his family lived comfortably. He had a rich garden that wound down to the river which yielded greens and staples not easy to come by and he had that most rare of possessions in the Soviet Union: he had servants, two of them, who looked after his house and his gardens.

Ivan Russitch by no means suffered under the yoke of repression either psychologically, emotionally, or financially. He had little reason to yearn for the freedom that was about to be thrust upon him. He was one of the inheritors of the good Soviet life. He was an *apparatchik*.

But Ivan Russitch was to discover that his guilty past, kept hidden and under control for all of his life, was to become a mechanism of distress as he struggled with a secret life that welcomed the freedoms offered, just as the Russitch in him tried to reject them.

Ivan Russitch had been born Isaak Reshevsky. Ivan Russitch had been born a Jew.

In the paranoia and confusion of the Patriotic War with Germany, Isaak had been able to change his name and escape, he thought, his patrimony. The change was allowed by the state as a gesture for his loyalty to the motherland and in the ensuing decades the *apparat* had, by accident or design, managed to forget who Isaak, now Ivan, really was.

He climbed the ladder of privilege through very hard work, dedication to the Party and his natural born smarts. He was at the epitome of his career—just before freedom struck.

When we arrived, so that there would be no confusion on the subject, we announced ourselves as capitalists, Americans and Jews. Our loud announcement took the sting out of the suspicious rumors that we were all three and were proud of it. Suspicions were laid to rest. Truth and acknowledgement replaced rumor.

It was at this time that Russitch, already bedeviled by the realization that gates to Israel were creaking open, confessed his terrible secret to us. His heritage, forgotten and fallow, emerged from the shadows and he discovered after decades the terrible itch to become again what he had always been—a Jew with his own homeland.

We urged him to come out of his Jewish closet and we helped the process along when Russitch shyly asked us to lead a Passover service for his family. They had heard of Passover, mostly at Easter time when the pogroms had previously come at the behest of the paranoically anti-semitic Stalin.

Russitch and his family began to sense from what spiritual riches they had turned away. They began to long for 'belonging' and for the warmth and emotional safety of their own society. They discovered, to their enormous surprise, that they had had enough of separation and denial.

The Passover service quickly melted their few remaining ties to a political system that denied their Jewishness. There were tears, not only among the family, but real heaves of sadness and joy among those of us who reached into their own childhood for the tales and tunes, dimly remembered. The Seder was that special moment when history and humanity meld into one.

Russitch, now again Reshevsky, and his small and bewildered clan, gave up their privileges, turned their back on their hard won fortune and security, and put themselves into our hands.

Emigrating from the U.S.S.R. at that time still took months and years of dangerous negotiation and expensive permits. The hated Jew, so long having deceived the state, was not to escape so easily . . . or, perhaps, at all. Russitch, now Reshevsky, having cut his ties to his past, found himself and his family with little future.

But we had a sailboat, we were Americans, and we

were, the most UNLIKELY combination, Jews and sailors. With us in his pocket Reshevsky became uncharacteristically brave and audacious. He would, he declared, run away on our boat, if we would have him and his clan, and be carried to Israel.

Our hand had been truly called. What had been an easy exhort on our part now became a dangerous game of escape. We were hoist by our own petard and, if truth be known, we gloried into the rarefied air of conspiracy against an enemy of our people.

Bringing them, one by one, aboard was easy since there had developed a great traffic between Odessa and UNLIKELY. Clearing customs and the police was the danger but, being in a poverty-stricken country, we treated the officials so well that only a cursory glance at our papers as we sat in their offices brought out the yearned-for stamps and signatures.

We sailed out of Odessa, late one dark night, laden with illegal supercargo. We started to breathe only after we passed the mouth of the Danube that divides Russia from Bulgaria.

We sailed through the Bosphorus whose buildings and bridges and obvious wealth brought gasps from our passengers and then into the curiously accommodating arms of the Turks, abetted by a call to and from the Israeli consulate.

Paperwork accomplished, not without some bad moments, the worst of which was the need to prove to the Israelis that the Russitchs, now Reshevskys, were truly Jews. Through luck and legerdemain the deeds were done and we saw the little band of no longer Russitch *emigrés* depart on an El Al flight to Tel Aviv.

Long afterwards, as we progressed on our circumnavigation, a postcard caught up with us. The front was a picture of the ancient gates of Jerusalem. On the back was the terse message,

"Life is hard . . . but we are free!"

The Reshevskys were learning to breathe the searing oxygen of freedom.

THE RUSSIAN WHO LOVED ARIZONA

They had no English but they did have a piece of paper from which they were preparing to read. It was dark and in the unlit marina in Odessa I could not make out who they were when they came aknocking on my hull.

"Hello Sasha," I called, thinking that they were some of the folk from the Seamen's club. The callers were uncomfortable to begin with; being addressed in English almost sent them scurrying back into the dark shadows of the hardstand through which they had appeared.

"Sasha? Is that you, Sasha?" No reply save some indistinct mumbles. I realized finally that it was not Sasha. Out of the murk and the mumble I was able to hear what sounded, distantly, like English. It was ten at night and I had had a difficult day trading my seven words of Russian for the twenty five words of English that was the vocabulary of most of the sailors in the marina. How to get rid of them quickly was all I could think about. A warm and welcome bunk was waiting and these two wanted to palaver in a language they did not know and in an accent I could hardly understand.

But I was their guest. My boat was the first western 'pleasure yacht' (the officials did not know what else to call us) to ever make port at Odessa. I felt obligated to be at least as nice as my Russian hosts had been to me.

"Come on aboard," I called. They carefully negotiated the gangplank and, in the cold wet of a March night on the Black Sea, they took off their shoes and trouped below.

I was delighted to see that they were not carrying the

obligatory bottle of vodka that appears as oil for all social intercourse. Vodka, and hospitable, welcoming Russians had laid my crew low more than once in the few days we had been here. At least they did not want to drink into dawn and semiconsciousness. The Russians have a phenomenal capacity and I have none.

We draped ourselves about the pilot house and after a few *spassibos* and many smiles the paper came out and its message, so carefully crafted by an English translator, was delivered and read with a heavy Russian accent.

"At one P.M., on this Saturday next our new boat into the water is put. We shall place on her the name at that time."

I acknowledged the news, still puzzled and awaited more. The two, one young boy and the other, a tall and balding sailor with a weathered face, smiled and addressed themselves again to the paper.

"When into the water our boat goes we shall name her." Full stop. I nodded and waited. "You, my dear and honored captain, shall christen her for us. You, dear Sir, will honor us and our new boat to be the godfather." With that they both rose and made a small bobbing bow while spreading their arms outward from their body, palms up, in a swimming gesture all the while ducking their heads in imitation of the bobbing bow of their bodies. It was an altogether startling act of contrite obeisance . . . as if the request was simply too much to ask. The little dance said that they would understand if I curtly refused and chased them out into the dark.

I was stunned. It was a scene out of Gogol with peasants seeking approval of the master for a newborn son. The gestures ill fitted the world of socialist equality in which my Russian supplicants had been reared. Ancient habits die hard.

Curiously, the night turned soft, made light by the warmth and the truth of their need. A yellow moon appeared and borne on the dying wind a whiff of incense, as from a high church altar, came from the two sailors. They were remaking unpleasant reality with only half remembered incantations. They had called up a structured, magical, past.

The godfather is chosen for real, imagined, or mystical powers so that he may intervene with the gods in favor of the new child. It was a gesture as ancient as the earth of old Russia. Seventy years of Marxism and a thousand of Christianity drifted away as I felt the pull of archaic belief.

They must have taken my silence, born of surprise, as the commencement of a refusal. They shuffled and made as if to leave, hurriedly, from the embarrassment of having troubled me. I was searching for the word and gesture that would repay the drama they had brought. I was not of their time or of their place. I had no memory of a hundred generations of serfdom only recently overlaid with a more modern and less gentle servitude. I did not know how to return the bow with the correct mode of acceptance. I grinned like a mime trying to appease an audience, nodded vigorously and, in English which of course they did not understand, I said, "I'll bring the champagne."

The launching, the christening, was a joy. Friends and distant relatives, representatives of the sailing club to which he had for so many years belonged, mothers and fathers all hummed with excitement. The fullness of pleasure banked the cold wind and eked a bit of reluctant sunlight from the northern sky. The smiles of the onlookers and the sense that now finally it was their time filled the dockside as the little boat, a quarter tonner, crouched a bit fearfully under the looming crane. This was the sailor's biggest day capping three thousand days of grayness and despair.

The last time the sailor had been given a boat amid the shortages of Soviet life was ten years before, when he had earned the right to skipper an ancient and creaky wooden boat hardly able to sail out of its own wake. She was, ten years ago, a thing of intense beauty and light amid the despair of the time. The sailor was offered the choice of a new name for her, the planning committee being doctrinally unsuperstitious about renaming boats.

"Arizona. I want to name her Arizona," was his instant, thoughtless, automatic response ten years ago.

"Arizona?" the chairman sputtered, "Arizona? An American state. You want to name a Soviet boat after an American state!" The sailor suddenly realized the enormity of the gaffe. Even his chance of getting the boat hung in the balance.

"Ha! ha! A small joke, Mr. Chairman. Of course we shall name her Stalina." And so she carried that name till Gorbachev loomed out of the Chekhovian mists of the Kremlin when Stalina became Perestroika.

But now ten years later, a new planning committee, infected with the delirious whiff of freedom that Gorbachev had brought, recognized the years of service of this sailor by assigning him the first small Polish sailboat to come into Odessa. The crane dipped the perky vessel into the water, the cheers rang out, and the godfather, bearing gifts of charts and sailing books (in English, alas) was warned that he must not strike the little vessel with the champagne lest he damage her. The cork popped on good Odessa champagne and the ARIZONA, for so she was named after ten years of waiting, slid off like an eel into a spanky breeze that might have given lesser sailors pause.

Later over too many vodkas and with the help of a Russian friend who had good English, I asked the question which had burned in me since the beginning of the drama.

"Why, my Russian friend, why Arizona? Why Arizona ten years ago when it was dangerous and why Arizona now when your country has freedoms enough to name ten thousand boats?"

The sailor smiled. The story, he said, started back in the bleak and cold steppes of eastern Russia. He had been brought up there, on a collective farm, and he never, in his entire youth, ever remembered being warm. Then, somewhere in a book, he read of hot, dry and sunny Arizona . . . the opposite ends of creation from the cold wet winds of his steppe. Arizona became his picture of heaven. The sailor fell in love with the heat, the sun, and finally with the curious sonority of the word itself.

"No politics, my American friend, nothing to do with America, nothing to do with our Marxist difficulties." And here the yearning look spread over his face no longer able to fully dream the dreams of youth, "No, I just came to be in love with Arizona as a young man might fall in love with a maid. I was seduced by the thought of the soft and sensuous feel of Arizona's sand and the warmth, as from a woman's body, of her sun.

"Ah, Arizona, Arizona!"

The sailor sighed that huge, full sigh of which only Russians seem capable and wandered off into the cold rain to commune with his boat. The clouds parted for an instant and a shaft of Arizona sunlight, half a world out of place, settled around his shoulders, toasting this happy sailor.

CHAPTER FOUR

Bad People

EVEN THE BAD FOLK you meet at sea somehow leaven their evil ways with a touch of common humanity. All of us are, more or less, bad people. All of us receive better than we deserve. If we all got what we deserved we would all hang.

The evil in ourselves is best recognized when we rub up against truly evil people. They are the mirror into which we look and see some of them in us. Perhaps other people's evil keeps most of us at least moderately good.

Ziggy was the lowest of all creatures and he declared it. The mayor was worse because he pretended not to be evil and the poor assistant harbormaster had not a clue that his actions were egregious.

In a strange way I loved Ziggy for his openness, his fierce, if misguided, loyalty and I felt sympathy for the assistant harbormaster in his incredible innocence.

I truly hated only the mayor.

ZIGGY

I never knew a less admirable human being nor, at the same time, a more admirable shipmate. When I met him, Ziggy was on the run from the Spanish government for desertion from the Spanish Foreign Legion. He had joined that curious unit to escape from the German government to whom he admitted owing a very large amount of taxes. I suspect that the tax problem was only the tip of an iceberg of peccadilloes, in which was embedded a hint of murder, because Ziggy, the eeliest of types, would have neatly slithered out of so small a contretemps as a taxation problem.

Ziggy was primal. His every instinct, his every response, were an immediate manning of the ramparts. He was a survivor in a world that had dealt him lousy cards which, it must be admitted, he played badly.

Ziggy could read, about a page a day, but only sappy love and adventure novels printed in large type. In the time I knew him he never read, or even glanced at, a newspaper. His world, that which was directly about him, was tactile: that which he could touch, he knew. Everything beyond the reach of his senses was a gray fog which held neither threat nor promise for him. Politics, art, literature, and history were not even words in his vocabulary.

Ziggy was blond and his judgment of folk was on a descending scale of whiteness and distance from Germany. Anyone less blond was suspect. Dark skins were 'monkeys', Italians being dark skinned were dismissible, the English made 'rubbish', the French were lousy engineers. Women were an unmentionable word and existed solely for his pleasure and use. He must have been a creative lover because, despite his despicable nature, his retinue of young, obedient, and nubile females was impressive.

Ziggy gave no one his permanent allegiance. For short

periods he would rent his loyalty out but the lease was easily and frequently cancelled. He was a liar, a cheat, a
scoundrel, a thief and, if truth be known, more likely than
not a murderer, a pedophile, and a pederast.

But all that was ashore. The moment Ziggy stepped
onto a sailboat he was the best shipmate I have ever
known. He became intensely loyal to the boat and his
skipper while at sea and would fight off attacks, both financial and physical, with unmeasurable intensity. He was
gentle with most crew and refrained from the more ob-
scene four letter words while untied from dock. In port,
however, all restraints were off.

Ziggy was a dream in any emergency. He was fright-
eningly strong, and would put his strong body at risk without a thought to self. He was an instinctive sailor and
brutally creative as a mechanic. Engines did not last long
around Ziggy but when needed, they ran . . . cowered a
bit, but ran.

His touch on a tiller was as gentle as his view of the
world was fierce. Ziggy, stateless and without a passport,
knew that the only place in the world in which he could be
free was in a sailboat, away from tormentors (and tor-
mentees) who confused and confounded his limited grip
on reality.

Ziggy came to me in Djibouti, rowing over from a
boat on which he had just arrived. He could no longer accept the errors and the egregiousness of his drunken, landlubberly skipper and, without papers, he could not even go
ashore. Ziggy needed passage to the Mediterranean on a
small sailboat free of the close scrutiny of officialdom. I
was his only hope, the only sailing vessel in Djibouti going
north.

I took him on and he re-stepped my broken 55-foot
mast almost with his own strength alone. He kept my reluctant engine going in the turbulence of the Red Sea and
he caged free fuel and supplies from beer buddies on oil
rigs on the way north. Ziggy saved my life and my boat

more than once and served with cheerful selflessness all the time he was aboard.

I agreed to take him to Israel where the Israelis, with their deep sensitivity to statelessness, allowed him entrance. Someone sold him an engineless, mastless, sailless wreck of a wooden 21-foot sloop for which Ziggy promised to pay a huge sum with his labor over a protracted period. I pointed out that he was being cheated by the price but Ziggy shrugged and went on rebuilding his frail craft with whatever inadequate materials and equipment he could beg, borrow or, as it proved, steal. Ziggy, who had always held the world at ransom, was, it seemed, getting his comeuppance.

One dawn we awoke to find Ziggy, his latest lady slave, and the little engineless boat gone. In the night he had slipped his lines and drifted quietly in a most seamanlike fashion through the tight noose of security that the Israelis have thrown around their beleaguered nation. He left behind him numerous folk who, secure in Ziggy's lack of a passport or a seaworthy vessel, thought that their property was safe with him. They underestimated his seamanship.

Ziggy had found a way, the only way, to survive in a world where people, *sans* passports, were fair game for any petty policeman. Ziggy knew, as those of us who in other contexts take to the sea know, that only at sea, needing only the winds, was he ever again to be his own man.

With no papers and an absolutely unseaworthy 21-foot wooden wreck he escaped to sea.

Some months later I sailed from Israel and made port in the harbor of Larnaca on Cyprus. As I pulled in a familiar blond sailor waved to me from the dock. Ziggy, in his impossible little boat had made the first leg of his passage to freedom. I was delighted.

I leaned across the bow and called out, "Hey Ziggy! Terrific! Glad to see you."

Ziggy grimaced, glanced conspiratorially around, cupped his hands and in a stentorian stage whisper called back hoarsely,

"D o n 't . . . c a l l . . . m e . . . Z i g g y ! !"

THE MAYOR OF SAN FRANCISCO BAY

I have always been fascinated with the strange routes by which sailors come to the sea. Some come voluntarily, seeking broader horizons and adventure, some are driven by the need to escape the unpleasantness of land, and some, a minority it is hoped, are forced to sea by an inability to maintain the level of incivility that the crush of land requires.

For all, no matter whence came the push, the sea provides a haven. But the sea is especially important to those who, because they find themselves in adversarial, warlike combat with their fellows, escape their social failures on land by going to sea where temper and intransigence find few targets and generate little opposition.

Mike was one of these contentious few. I met Mike pushing his recently acquired boat along the southern coast of Turkey. The initial hint of a flawed personality came with our first beer when he described how he had responded with abuse to an alleged overcharge at a Turkish restaurant. Since Turkey is the cheapest place in the western world, or at least it was then, I thought that perhaps poor Mike had been unlucky enough to fall into one of the few tourist traps in that lovely country. As the story developed he had not. It became obvious, as I got to know Mike better, that if anyone fell into a trap it was more likely the Turkish restaurateur than Mike.

I asked my usual question that I put to new sailors I meet. How had he come to the sea? The tale he told me, a fascinating one, was strangely unconnected, as if important events had been omitted that did not bear retelling.

Mike had retired from business at fifty, a too early age for a driven and passionate man as I came to know Mike. He hinted that his partner, in self-defense, had either forced him to sell or bought him out of his business at a very good price. Mike was vague as to why he had left the business world. Curiously, his next move was right back into business via a piece of property he owned in one of those villages named after sharks and Spanish saints that ring the upper reaches of San Francisco Bay. The residents of the little town upon which Mike descended were busy defending, in communal manner, rampant urbanization. They informed Mike that his property could not be built upon as it was being reserved for park land and would be bought from him at a fair price. The 'no' rankled Mike on principle. It did not matter to Mike that the eventual benefit to him from the buy out would far outweigh any profit he might earn from building on the land. The red flag of opposition was waved and, unable to respond in any other manner, Mike went to war.

Eighteen months later he emerged with a license to build and, in the process, he destroyed the development plan that had taken a decade of work. In his own words he "had learned so much about politics and had made so much noise and commotion" that, in one of the more arcane accidents of American politics, he ran for and was elected mayor of the town. As Mike described it, his four-year term was hell for him. One can only surmise the kind of difficulties he raised for his constituents who came quickly to recognize that power elevated his prickliness to the level of pure abuse.

At the end of the four years Mike had had enough. "Politics is a process," he said, "where you only end up making everybody unhappy." Since politicians are generally known for their craven passion to please everyone,

Mike, who ended up scratching his fingernails across the slates of everyone in town was, as a politician, the screaming exception.

In Mike's defense it must be said that his community was not your regular little old middle class American town. A well-known preaching philosopher ensconced in a houseboat lead the fight of the house boaters. His forces were arrayed against powerful developers. The homosexual community was beginning to feel its political oats and exercise its muscle. The old time residents of the sleepy little fishing village—that the place had once been—were outraged by everything that was happening and malignantly suspicious, not without cause, of all these strange folk who had rushed in to disturb their ancient rhythms.

Furthermore, a remnant of San Francisco's less reputable Mauve Decade had been mayor before him and nobody in town, except the fire department people who adored her, was altogether happy about having the most famous Madame in the West as their chief executive.

Into this turmoil Mike introduced his own special brand of peremptory intemperance. Things became so bad, Mike recalls proudly, that at one point his opponents, outraged by his highhandedness, put the rule of law behind them and, in a draconian gesture, burned down a condominium development that he was building. They felt that the mayor had, to put the best face on the matter, used venal political muscle to obtain the building variances which allowed the development to go forward. Mike does not deny this.

It was at this point, when the attacks against him from all sides gained strength, that Mike decided that discretion was the better part of valor and he hastily took to the sea. As crew he signed on (some said seduced) a former friend's wife, a nice lady whose special pleasure seemed to be the abuse that she received from Mike in all matters. Had he tied her to the mast and beat her with sail battens it would have been kinder for her and certainly easier on the sensibilities of visitors to their boat. As it was, the embarrassment that strangers felt in the presence of Mike's endless vocal persecution of the mild, doelike creature was intense. After a while, folk Mike met en route just faded away, exhausted by the effort to maintain strained smiles during Mike's attacks on a lady who could not or would not defend herself.

Mike's temper lay just below the surface and would emerge at the slightest confront behind a gritted teeth smile that fooled no one. To any sort of opposition, Mike tossed over his shoulder as he walked away, an unanswerable, "Do what you gotta do," a comment which laid out Mike's unconcern for your position and his disinclination to even discuss it with you. You were left choking with unuttered responses.

Mike's solution to the mountains of opposition that he left strewn about the landscape had been to hie for the seas where there were fewer folk to confront and fewer past enemies to deal with. At sea his temper could be freely exercised on a docile mate too small and weak to fight back. At sea he was free of the inclination of exasperated colleagues to put rule of law aside once more and go at Mike with pickax handles. It must be admitted that his run for the sea was an intelligent decision; one that, it can be argued, Mike took just in time.

While, for the most part, the sea shielded Mike from the worst effects of his temper, there came a time when even the sea seemed to have enough of him. We had coasted along together for a few days and had come at sundown into a quiet cove. Mike invited me to raft alongside which I proceeded to do. It had become dark and the testy winds of Turkey chose that moment to pipe up. Rafting sailboats, even in a daylight calm, is tricky business and I was not deft enough, in Mike's opinion, at the process. It became clear that the maneuver was going badly and Mike's temper started to mount. He became furious at the effrontery of the wind and at my inability, in the lowering storm, to respond to his shouted and insulting directions. Finally he reached his limit and without a word he cast me off in the dark to fend for myself on a close shore that I did not know. I managed to get an anchor down before going aground and watched Mike's stern light disappear around the point into the teeth of a building *meltemi*.

He was by this time in such a fury that he needed to make a gesture of total rejection—which in this instance meant abandoning me no matter how uncomfortable it might be for him. It was a process that he must have repeated compulsively and helplessly with others in his long history of high dudgeon. So off he went and ran immediately into nasty winds and unpleasant seas that cast him back ignominiously. He was rejected by the very sea in which he had sought revenge on me.

For Mike this was a bitter pill. Not only did he have to run for shelter but he had to share his shelter with me whom, I am sure, he blamed for the wind and perhaps with some logic for his difficulties. In order to placate him, if only for his lady's sake, I called on VHF and offered to stand anchor watch for both of us so that he could get some sleep.

There was a long pause and then he treated me and my offer with his bitter, disinterested "Do what you gotta do," and snapped off the radio in a gesture of total dismissal. I was left clutching a dead microphone and trying unsuccessfully to clutch at my temper and to find a reason to excuse such churlishness.

The last time I saw Mike was in the lovely named port of Marmaris, where yachts from all over the world are lined up chock-a-block for a mile along the quay. I had come in first and was able to hold on to a few feet next to me for Mike, who asked to tie up alongside. Marmaris is a Mediterranean mooring which means that you drop an anchor off your bow a hundred feet out and back up into any sliver of space that appears possible, which is all there ever is along those crowded shores. Mike sent his lady out to the bow to drop the anchor but he had forgotten to tie off his dinghy alongside. As a result, when Mike started to back down and gave the curt order to drop anchor to his already terrified and bemused lady, the dinghy had drifted forward and lay nestled under the bow where she could not see it.

"Now!" bellowed Mike, "drop it now . . . fast . . . get it down, now!" The lady tried to remonstrate, to tell Mike that there might be a problem at the bow, but he became violent and screamed at here, "Now, God-dammit, now you stupid bloody cow!" The lady shut up, took one more look over the bow, and as Mike continued to scream at her did as she was ordered. The chain sang out of the locker pulled by a 60-pound plow which did not even hesitate as it went through the bottom of the dinghy.

There was dead silence for only a moment as the shattered dinghy and its new outboard came to rest in thirty feet of water. The lady glanced at the ruined dinghy, her face curiously at ease as Mike's howls of abuse were heard along the quay by sailors of a hundred nations. She sat quietly, almost triumphantly on the bowsprit, not even trying to point out, as if that would have made any difference, that she was only doing as he had screamingly ordered.

She was immediately banished from the boat and sent home to America the same day.

Lucky lady.

THE ASSISTANT HARBORMASTER

In a land where anyone would do anything for a buck, the assistant harbormaster of Hurghada would do anything for a dime.

All of us have suffered from the universal discomfiture of falling into the hands, in foreign ports, of minor officialdom. In most cases a small bribe will do. In Colombia they wanted my entire boat, and in Hurghada, on the Egyptian coast of the Red Sea, the assistant harbormaster (one of many) was well into destroying my milk of human kindness before, providentially, a wonderful riposte occured to me.

Hurghada is a developing touristic dive harbor aimed at the exploitation of the wonderful coral reefs of the northern part of the Red Sea. The location and access to the reefs are superb, but, alas, this is accompanied by access to arriving boats by minor officials bent on regaining with unseemly haste the price they paid for the office they had purchased from officials slightly above them.

The reason for the haste is that in Egypt, as in other shores of the lesser blessed world, one never knows when the official one flight up will be replaced with a new one, who himself paid slightly more for office than his predecessor. The new purchaser will have his own list of wannabe folk to whom offices will be sold out from under of, and with little warning to, the present office-holders.

It was into a pair of oily hands, the owner of which had just made his purchase of office, that we were delivered when we arrived at Hurghada with salt watered batteries and starter motor. We were Prime Grade A grist for the assistant harbormaster's extraction machine since we needed parts and labor and all sorts of purchasable mandatory permissions in order to get on our way.

The assistant harbormaster had his golden goose. He was smart enough to pluck each feather, one at a time, slowly (since he could delay our departure endlessly) rather than to kill the opulent creature. Milk, do not slaughter, was his motto.

The moment soon came when we could no longer abide by the milking process. Almost better to be slaughtered than to continue, egregiously, to be forced to offer our rich, western teat to the assistant harbormaster's bottomless appetite.

We were not a boat, we were not people, we were a very large dollar sign and he had a narrow and determinate period in which to operate on us.

He started with the usual. A pack of American cigarettes. Then a carton. Food. Then in a day or two as we chafed to be on our way, all of our cigarette stores. Then alcohol with each request accompanied by the assurance that this was his last. The day came when he extracted a portable radio and two pair of binoculars. After which, when he had determined that we could no longer safely spare supplies or equipment he got serious in the field of cash. He was clearly out to get it all.

There was, however, a chink in his armor. The first day he came aboard he inspected the two women crew with a frank, almost stated, interest in their availability. His chink was his rampant sexuality accompanied by his sure knowledge that women were only good for one thing and here he had two western (read highly desirable) women somewhat at his mercy.

I quickly made it clear that my wife was neither for sale nor for rent but we had a problem with the other couple who were not married nor sexually intertwined. Just two very good friends from New Zealand who loved each other's company, if not each other.

When this unheard of platonicism was monosyllabically explained to the assistant harbormaster his eyes widened with disbelief and in amazement at the strange ways of the West.

"You mean," he inquired aghast at the thought, "you mean he does not 'use' her?"

This was my first inkling that we might be able to do the dirty to the assistant harbormaster, without having to give up either our women or any more of our goods.

One of the matters in which he had expressed interest, to my puzzlement, was in our medical supplies. Endless questions concerning our ability to cure or alleviate this or that ill, all unrelated to himself, but all clearly involving a personal agenda.

Sure enough, the day, the great day for which we had prayed, arrived. One morning he requested a private audience with me. His hemming and hawing were epic and his paralytic inability to get to the point was tiring both of us. I tried to walk away but each time a sadness came over him, so unlike his usual demeanor, that, if only out of curiosity, I sat and waited him out.

The wait was hugely rewarded.

"You see," he said hesitantly, "I strong man. I use women all my life. I have wife I use. I have girls I use and, and . . . " his voice trailed of in palpable embarassment.

"Yes," I said, trying to hide my unbecoming pleasure in his anguish, "yes, please go on."

"You see," his throat knotting with confession, "you see, I now, lately, for a little time," and here he took a great breath and blurted out, "have great diffiulty making use . . . you know . . . my manhood does not . . . react."

"How can we help?" I said almost but not quite feeling sorry for him.

"Well . . . perhaps great American medicine has cure. In your medicine box perhaps a pill or an ointment that will," his wretchedness was overwhelming, "give me back my man."

Gotchya, I said to myself. Gotchya you greedy, graspy snake. Gotchya by your soft and inadequate snakiness. Ha!!

"Why yes, we do have exactly what you need. But it is awfully expensive . . . much more than you can afford."

His eyes moist with yearning and anticipation of his good fortune he screeched, "Anything, just ask."

"Too much money, but . . ." I hesitated.

"Yes, yes."

"Perhaps if you can make things easier for us, faster and less demanding, perhaps . . ."

"Yes, yes, yes. I understand. No more baksheesh, no more permissions, no more anything."

At this point I bade him to return tomorrow but, on pain of denial of the potion, he was not to mention the matter to anyone.

Off he went. Now I had the problem of producing an impossible medicine. I went below and surveyed my supplies. The only thing that came close was a jar of vaseline. I carefully removed the label, scraped the printing off the metal lid and spent the next two hours hand printing the following message:

American Sex Cream
Use immediately before intercourse
Approved by the AMA, USDA, ADA, ABA,
and all other sexually oriented organizations

It was a masterpiece.

The following day I covertly delivered the jar into his sweating hands and received his guarantee that, work or not, we would have no further trouble from him.

Two days passed and no assistant harbormaster. On the third day he showed up barely able to drag himself up the gangplank, so exhausted was he.

We feared that we had overplayed our hand until, down in the cabin where no one could hear, he told his story.

"American Sex Cream magnificent. I fuck for two

days with wife and all night with many very surprised ladies. My man never failed due to magical cream."

Tears of gratitude rolled down his cheeks.

And, and this did not discomfit us, he had the last laugh on folk who had tried to diddle him.

The last I heard, he was screwing his way through phalanxes of appreciative females and in his gratitude American boats henceforward were off baksheesh limits in the port of Hurghada.

CHAPTER FIVE

Off The Wall People

NOT GOOD, NOT BAD, just plain awesome.
Herein are remembered folk who push the envelope of 'normalcy' while remaining clear and rational . . . in their own terms. 'Their own terms' best describes how these people can live in an atmosphere of high, exciting drama and, in their deviations, teach the rest of us how life could be.

Here are folk who put passion first and reason last. Their lives instruct us that reason, pure or otherwise, is simply not the perfect paradigm for human beings.

All hail the goofy, balmy, loony, wacky and zany folk who cause even the gods to laugh.

THE ADAMANT ARYAN AND THE TOTALLY HERBAL DUO

Given the exigencies of acquiring sailing crew, skippers will sign on almost anything but a gorilla. (Gorillas are signed onto racing boats.) The resulting mixed bag is often the ruination of passages. Not because that crew might be bad, lazy or evil, but simply that they are different. Different from you and different from each other.

Take for example this most rampant case of polarity

which descended on me recently. Coming up the Red Sea, a confront in itself, I found myself sailing with a pair of unmixable extremes, the adamant Aryan versus the totally herbal duo.

The adamant Aryan was an archetypal Goth who had no opinions that were not black or white and no preferences that were not German. His education was limited to knowing the prices of everything. Of what made the world work he knew nothing and cared less. He had a brutal interest in females, but a glass of beer or a recalcitrant diesel immediately superceded women. He was blank on women's liberation, it simply did not parse. Homosexuality was beyond the pale, not for him or any healthy man, "*Nein! nein!* not for me, *absolut.*"

He knew nothing of politics, art, or history and cared not a whit that he did not. Anything he disagreed with, and the list was long, was either 'rubbish' or 'shtupid'.

His favorite food was meat. He once found himself in North Africa, meatless, and was tempted to eat, as some North Africans do, monkey brains. But his finer nature intervened and he refrained in spite of his meat hunger because, as he so unforgettably put it, "It vould be like eating mine liddle bruder." Except for his little brother, and possibly even other close blood relatives, any meat would do, anything that had walked about on its own was acceptable grist for his sausages. Salads were 'cow food'. Among those acceptable gustatory objects that did not perambulate on their own, only the potato existed.

Anyone less white than he was less human. Consideration for others was built on a descending scale from pale to less pale. Even among the paler peoples he churned out preferential sorts. White was Northern Europe. Spain, Italy and the like, were too close to tan to be taken seriously. Besides they were 'shtupid' engineers. He had nothing bad to say about Scandinavians but nothing really good either as he considered them not sufficiently aggressive. He hated the French; they were bad soldiers. He had a grudging respect for the English, "but their engineers make British rubbish." The Chinese, the Japanese, and the Indians were 'monkeys' and all Africans were subhumans on whom any kindness and all assistance was wasted.

He abused himself with alcohol and tobacco. His coughing in the morning was wet and corosive and he smelled, on a vessel of non smokers, like tobacco rot.

To the adamant Aryan the world was a movable garbage pail. His great joy was to dispose of trash wherever he happened to be, with keen and evident pleasure if it mucked up some third world beach. Even nuclear waste was acceptable. Oil spills and mercury did not interest him. He regretted the loss of an animal species only when its disappearance deprived him of another meat to eat. He would kill an elephant for a sandwich or a whale for the lamp oil to eat it by. He expressed an interest in tasting porpoise.

He loved to shoot guns and sharpen knives.

Get the picture?

Wait till you hear about the others.

The totally herbal duo were a pair of young New Zealanders who stood morally above and outside of our familiar universe. They were our consciences imposed upon us by superior folk. They were the high standards of concern and sensitivity to which the future would surely rise. They were threatening the rest of us, Michelangelo's Christ in Judgment on the far wall of the Sistine Chapel. But the totally herbal duo lacked the opiate of faith which lay behind the judgments of Jesus.

Their belief was in themselves, their opinions of goodness and justice, and their profound conviction that all personkind (their word) were redeemable. What was needed to solve the world's ills were good intentions and the intervention of the enlightened (themselves) West in the affairs of the Third World and other worlds whose sad condition was, "after all, our doing anyway." They accepted moral guilt for all things, perhaps even the Big Bang.

The herbal duo were truly herbal. Not even an egg could be ingested and they had been known to occasionally use surgical masks to prevent the accidental taking of endangered insect life. Meat was a four letter word. They were as nauseated by watching the eating of meat as by the motion of the boat itself. They suffered from acute *mal de viande*.

The mere thought of putting teeth into formerly living flesh revolted them and raised their herbal needs to even higher levels. Grains were their staple with the infrequent addition of a mushroom, although the too close association of mushrooms with flesh made them feel daring.

They celebrated all living things that fit the mold of their conviction. They played music to plants and shielded trees by the side of the road from abuse.

They loved the black races for their 'childlike inadequacies'. The blacker, the more inadequate and the more benighted, the better. They sought, with their own labor and spirit, to protect starving Africans from abusing each other and suffering abuse from the outside world. They wanted, needed, yearned to be of service to the common-person (their word). Their yearning set them aside, made them, in their eyes, admirably uncommon. Absent a desperate horde of sufferers in need of ministering, they might well have created one. Or, at the least, unearthed undiscovered miseries requiring their sure, loving, and forgiving touch.

Tobacco was filth and disease—although, curiously, hashish was not. Alcohol, a product of their granary world, was enologically acceptable. Homosexuality had a quality of depressed nobility and there were always gay friends among their coterie, a conscious mix and balance to which they granted their herbal duo's seal of approval.

The *he* half of the duo saw himself as an artist, 'getting ready' to make great art. His favorites were "Dali and Rembrandt. Dali moves me very much." The *she* half, "little one," as he referred to her, espoused woman's lib. She was thoroughly and pointedly modern, becoming, however, de-liberate and quietly old fashioned with "her man." Art and music, poetry and literature rounded out their days. They were disgusted with television.

They understood all history perfectly. They knew exactly what the politicians should have done in the past and should be doing now. Clear and simple solutions could be achieved through clear and simple actions. It was all so obvious. They wondered how that which was so evident to them had escaped the notice of the leaders of the world.

Their most special crusade was the environment. The base line was how the physical world existed at their birth. Nothing should or could be changed on 'spaceship earth' from that marvelous moment. Nothing must be thrown into the sea. Trash, and even some garbage, was hoarded in month long passages to be carefully deposited upon reaching land. An aerosol can was an abomination. They had rules for living that made the four hundred proscriptions of the Koran seem simple.

During the occasional target practice with guns, the duo went screaming below, hands clapped to ears. A gun, any gun, was the ultimate obscenity, a too easy means of getting meat. It was the anathema of peace. Like politicians who are four square in favor of motherhood, they were four square in favor of peace.

Out of the self-perceived goodness of their hearts they were infinitely intolerant of others whose views of trash and violence deviated even a whit from their own. Color of inherited skin was acceptable. Color of personal beliefs was not.

Out of their passionate dedication to peace the duo finally reached a breaking point with the Aryan's dedication to guns and meat. On one sultry day in the Red Sea the conflict reached a point of no possible return. We could all see that the anger in the Aryan was fast approaching the release of physical violence to which he was, anyway, normally and easily inclined. The male half of the duo had little experience or desire for that kind of catharsis of combat and, for the female half, violence was, we all knew, unthinkable. So we waited for the Aryan to simply paste them both in the mouth and have done with it.

When the violence came it left the three of them and the rest of us in stunned disbelief. The nice little quiet girl, that unviolent, anti-war, prim and proper and wouldn't-hurt-a-fly person, simply hauled back and threw a straight right to the jaw of the Aryan. Whether from the force of the blow or from surprise, it decked him. As he recovered and stood up, rather thoughtfully it seemed, we all waited for the massacre.

He walked over to the ashen-faced girl, his six feet six towering over her five feet four, reached out, and gently plopped her into the calm sea. He did the same to the boy. While we, with some relief, hauled the totally herbal duo back on board, the Aryan nodded crisply to himself, went below, ate some meat and took a nap.

On land would I have made close friends with the adamant Aryan? Hardly. Would I have taken to my breast the manifest goodness of the flower children? In retrospect, I don't think so.

They were both all too sure of themselves. Too sure that they, each in their own way, had all the answers.

I didn't like the Aryan. When push came to shove I figured the world would deal with him.

On the other hand, folk like the duo, who have all the answers, make me really nervous . . . like Hitler did.

THE GONNA LIVE FOREVER GUYS

Over the years I have sailed with many an arcane crew-
man, but on a recent passage my shipmates, passionately
committed to health and long life via extreme diet and incessant exercise, sorely tested my love of fellow. I only survived because of a secret stash of Hershey bars that I had
smuggled aboard.

As skipper, I chose the dreaded 0300 to 0600 watch
so that, not surrounded as I was during the day by nutri-
tional nuts, the furtive unwrapping of my daily return to
reality by way of heavenly Hersheys would not generate
hoots of derision and predictions of an early and messy
death.

The five 'You Are What You Eat' boys also subscribed
to violent exercise of the 'No pain, no gain' school. With
Jesuitic fire and zeal, they proselytized fiercely, much like
a clutch of married women who can't abide the thought of
an unmarried male.

On a fifty-foot ketch passaging across the Atlantic for
the better part of a month, there was no escape for me. I
was thrust into the wonderland world of Alice, wherein
the Mad Hatter, the head nutritionist on the vessel, dashed
about checking his watch and intoning, "Eat this, do not
eat that!" The galley was littered with small vials that had
inscribed on them "Eat Me" or "Drink Me" (numbered
from 1 to 12, I'll never know why) and a special large jer-
oboam from which all aboard (save me) sucked a
'whammy', as they called it, at least once each day.

When I first heard talk about the whammy I had the
fleeting thought that, at least, there was some humor
aboard, some sense of the irrational road down which this
centenarily-directed clan was headed. But, alas, they were
serious about their whammies, a concoction imbibed as an
instant micro rejuvenator like the amphetamines of my
youth. I was quickly disabused of the thought that they
would do anything so gross and so destructive to their pre-

cious bodily fluids as to imbibe a chemical. The whammy was natural, a word I came to hate in spite of my early subscription to Mother Earth Catalog. Not only—they informed me from the enormous heights of their superior knowledge—would a whammy not hurt a fly, it would, indeed, lengthen the fly's life unto many generations and improve its fertility and sex life. Suppose, I shuddered, that some whammy accidentally did become available to the fly or cockroach population or, Heaven forfend, some hundreds of billions more of mosquitoes.

Worse than being up to our armpits in cockroaches was the prospect of billions more whammied people, all made to live longer with higher fecundity. We can't even handle the ones we got.

On land I would have long since faded away into a Baskin-Robbins or, out of pure spite, a Dunkin' Donuts. I would have run to the nearest 7-Eleven or bathed, perhaps, in Coke Classic to drown the guilt of oral suicide that I was committing upon myself with cholesterol and empty fats. But at sea I belonged to the believers. They had me. There was no place to run.

There was the matter of calisthenics. I have nothing against exercise. On a nice solid gym floor I have been known to do two, maybe three push ups and even five minutes of a pumpy, wheezy run. But calisthenics on a downwind fifty footer swaying from side to side like a crazed camel? I had trouble sitting still and these guys were on the foredeck lifting weights, doing push ups over the rail and, honest to gosh, organizing Thai kick-boxing matches.

A kick boxer spends a good deal of his time on one leg lashing out with his other. I needed four points of contact (two hands, two feet) with the lurcher (as the boat came to be called) and my shipmates were attempting it on one.

Had this passion for exertion stood alone it might not have been worth the telling but matched by the equally

passionate commitment to a mineral supplement diet requiring whammies and hourly sips of such delights as selenium and other rare earths, the passage was an event I
will never forget.

Prior to the ingestion of elements a test was per-
formed to measure the needs of the body. The test was so
direct, so self-evident and, as a result, so absurd that it
boggled the mind that they were being serious. I again sus-
pected that they were pulling an enormous and elaborate
practical joke on me. I could not accept that the daily
smelling of suspensions of these elements, selenium, cal-
cium, potassium, etc, would somehow signal the body's
needs.

But that was exactly what they believed. They sniffed,
they measured, they drank from "Drink Me" vials as, in
disbelief, I retreated ever farther into a Hershey bar.

I learned something about myself during this Wonderland passage: Better a Hershey bar, and perhaps an earlier demise, than selenium, whammies and push ups.

THE PROFESSOR DOCTOR

Everybody knows that, when it comes to matters of
health, Jews are just crazy. They make all their kids into
doctors and when, God forbid, they should need medical
advice themselves, only a specialist will do . . . maybe even
a professor.

So where did Israel's Premier, Itzhak Shamir, go when
he began feeling a little over-the-hill peckish? The Mayo
clinic? A monkey gland doctor in Switzerland? No. He
went to Romania. A nation so deeply mired in the nine-
teenth century that its dictator was still building castles for
himself.

Shamir and millions of less exalted folk have been
trekking to Bucharest for thirty years to fall under the spell

and receive the advice of Professor Doctor Ana Aslan. Professor Doctor (full title please, all the time) Ana Aslan is a spry chick of 91 years who could pass for a cute and sexy 60. But Professor Doctor Ana Aslan is more than just old. She is a serious scientist in her own right and by her own admission, who, for decades, had been dabbling in the elixirs of eternal life. Like Ponce de León, she sought the fountain of youth. Unlike that worthy Spanish explorer, she announced that she had found it.

And very convincingly too, if her roster of heads of state is any attestation. Indeed the Romanian government, which has dubbed Professor Doctor Ana Aslan a 'national treasure', is so enamored of her claims of longer life and demonstrations of greater health that they currently have 2,000,000 Romanians on her regimen and soon will have 70% of the entire population of Romania jumping through the hoops of Professor Doctor Ana Aslan. The Professor Doctor claimed to have done her first triple blind (ask your doctor) research project, thousand-cohort, year-long study of the effectiveness of her discovery in 1955 and, according to her figures—and who am I to doubt a Romanian statistic—she demonstrated a 21 percent drop in days lost from work due to illness, among the group that she treated, over those who were not treated. Impressive.

When I asked the Professor Doctor what message she would like me to carry back to America, she said, in her clear strong voice, "Tell your countrymen that Professor Doctor Ana Aslan wants all Americans to die healthy." Not a bad thought, that.

I'm no scientist and I have no medical bona fide so I have no intention of either making a judgment or, FDA forbid, a recommendation. But while I was nosing around Bucharest waiting to be received by the Professor Doctor, I did run across something that I am willing to recommend. In fact, if you are inclined to one of the more *outré* trips ever offered, and if you have no objections to having most of the cost picked up by Romania, this one might be for you.

Bucharest is no garden spot, in fact on a scale of one to ten as a swinging tourist spot, it comes up minus. The ambience is tones of gray, including that of most of the once exuberant and excitable Romanians. Except for the Intercontinental Hotel (good but far from *de luxe*) the rest, with one glorious exception, are well below the level of a Motel 6.

The glorious exception is the hotel where the Professor Doctor hangs out. It is the Flora Hotel, a small (200 rooms), immaculate and graceful hotel, three stories only and banded by cozy balconies. The dining room is like Paris (not the food, only the dining room) and the service, in 1990 when I was there, was unmarxist. It is set in a pleasant green park ten minutes from downtown Bucharest and if you have a room facing east you can discern in the distance the ugliest building in Europe. It is one of those wedding cake pastiches that Uncle Stalin gifted all over Eastern Europe to show how much was to be learned from Mother Russia. If you happen to be in the Flora in the summer the apparition is screened by trees, but if you can withstand the shock of so much concentrated hideous architecture, it is worth a special trip if only to see how wrong the old uncle could be.

But back to the Flora. Nothing here described concerning hotels cannot be found in any country in Europe, so what's the big deal?

The big deal is that the Romanian government, in a perfect proselytizing frenzy, and with an eye to the capture of hard currencies, has arranged for you to spend two weeks at the Flora Hotel, three meals a day, including air fare from and to the States for $1200. That's a big deal but, to be honest, not a really big deal.

The really big deal is that, included in the $1200, is a careful and extensive medical checkup, à la Mayo, from pate to toesies. Depending on what the doctors turn up there are specialists available, at no extra cost, for consultation. Additionally, at no extra cost, a trained dietitian makes a thorough review of your dietary and exercise habits. For two weeks you are placed (voluntarily, no one forces you) on a careful and tasty diet in the splendiferous dining room and, whether or not you choose to accept the advice offered, you have my guarantee that by simply eating better for two weeks, exercising sensibly and availing yourself of the massage rooms (included), the water therapy (included), and the spa (included), you will feel a damn sight better on leaving than you did when you arrived.

All of this activity takes place in a clinic appended by closed walkways to the Flora Hotel. You don't even have to step outside and risk a possibly fatal, distant glimpse of Uncle Joe's Folly. If you choose, you can spend a pampered and professional two weeks and hardly have to lift a finger.

But that can get pretty boring and, after all, you are in a new country and one rarely visited. All of the medical activity takes place in the mornings on weekdays. Afternoons and weekends are available, if you choose, for excursions and sightseeing (not included but so cheap that you'll think it's 1950).

Romania is one of those places where, within a few hundred miles, nature's extremes can be enjoyed. A few leagues to the east of your hotel is the Danube Delta on the Black Sea, a pristine nature preserve with animals and birds and an anarchy of flora in an untouched natural setting. A few leagues to the west, the Dolomites rise and enclose the Romanian mountain province of Transylvania. ("Yes, Virginia, there was a Count Dracula.")

Bucharest itself is not overwhelming. The architecture is dedicatedly *fin-de-siècle* French and the city has been little built upon or repaired since then. This lends an air of decayed and fallen aristocracy that is not at all unattractive.

I was on my way back to the hotel when an old chair in a window of a shop caught my eye. It was a piece of 30's junk, not worth a second thought but upholstered in a priceless piece of *Art Moderne* fabric. I bought the chair on the spot and, under the curious and disbelieving eyes of the shopkeepers, I denuded the wreck of its covering and left the chair for them to use as evidence that Americans are out of their minds.

Loaded with booty and a head full of arcane sights and places, you will, at the end of the cheapest two weeks imaginable, have your final consultation with the medical staff. The putative reason why you are in Romania in the first place is to receive advice which, they assure you, will enable you to live long and die healthy. The inevitable, immutable, and foreseeable result of the medical investigations of your body, no matter what your ills, will be their recommendation that you start taking *Aslavital* (named after you-know-who). These are little yellow 'miracle' pills which have never been known to harm anyone. *Aslavital* is the fifth generation elixir to be developed by the Professor Doctor, a year's supply of which is included in the tour package. No one says you have to take them, you are only obliged to listen to the Professor Doctor's advice. But, if you are curious, carry them home and ask your doctor.

Who knows? You might just live to a hundred, much to the confusion of your children.

Postscript: Shortly after my interview with the Professor Doctor she had the bad luck to die. This was a great shock to Romania since all expected that the Professor Doctor would break all records. It was a bad public relations blow to the Romanian balance of trade.

When I asked the Minister of Health what had happened, his answer was purest Romany.

"The Professor Doctor," this worthy announced to me, "was not supposed to die just yet."

"So what happened," I asked.

"Well, Sir, in the sense that she was not supposed to die we shall call her death accidental. She accidentally died before she was supposed to."

THE ICON SMASHER

There is something special about United States Marines. Having accepted discipline they know better than most how to deal with freedom. Phil is a retired Marine, a tough iconoclast best avoided by those prone to shovel cow chips. What is on Phil's mind is on his tongue, a condition guaranteed to both land him in the soup and reduce by a measurable degree the total volume of phony bombast in which we wallow.

Phil has been invited out of more marinas than any other sailor I know. He is a passionate enemy of injustice and has no fear of taking on City Hall as if it were no worse than the shores of Tripoli. Should a landlubber seek advantage over sailors, and Phil is within a thousand miles, he is the cavalry that comes roaring up.

But the thing that Phil hates worst is "pussyfooted two-facedness. A guy can do anything he wants, can say anything he wants just so long as it's for real," says Phil, "but when some jerk thinks he can bamboozle me with bullshit, watch out!"

I watched Phil in action in Cyprus one wonderful evening. There were about fifty American yachts at rest in the Larnaca marina under Phil's watchful and protective eye. Whatever happened to or about or by Americans was Phil's turf, so that when the local Lions (they have a Lion's Club in Cyprus) announced that a famous American astronaut, on tour from NASA, would speak, Phil recruited us all, had us don somewhat less smelly clothing than usual, and trooped us off to the meeting.

The talk went well, at the beginning. It was a straightforward and interesting account of training for space and dealing with space. We Americans were quietly, and properly, proud of this American's accomplishments.

Then the other shoe dropped. Our astronaut announced that he had had "a religious experience. I was born again in space."

Our Cypriot hosts squirmed in surprised embarrassment since religion is one of two forbidden subjects at Lion's meetings (the other being any mention of Turks). But as discomfited as the Cypriots were, the Americans in the audience were aghast. There was no way that the Cypriots could understand such a parochial and purely American phenomenon as being 'born again'. To our hosts, we all looked like foolish children. The astronaut invited his audience of Cypriots and Americans to share in his "great discovery of God." In another setting the discussion might have been interesting and rewarding. In a meeting room of Greek Orthodox Cypriots, to proselytize for born-again baptism was a disaster.

The talk over, the astronaut invited questions. The embarrassment and dismay were so deep that all we wanted, Americans and Cypriots alike, was to get out and away. But not Phil.

Out of his deep need to battle presumption, Phil rose in the stunned silence.

"Please, Sir," asked Phil with just the proper touch of asperity that old sergeants use toward young lieutenants, "please, Sir, would you mind telling us who is paying for your tour?"

With the smallest of pins he burst the balloon of tension and, in doing so, revealed the speaker not as a NASA scientist, as he had presented himself, but as a recruiter for his own brand of religion.

The evening was after all, especially for the Americans, a glorious success.

THE KANE MUTINY

Ed was no sailor. He became 65 and developed an unscratchable itch to put the world behind him. Ed was locked in by forces he himself had created. He was imprisoned by his own unstoppable urge for more and bigger businesses. Everything he touched grew, expanded, opened new horizons into which a lesser entrepreneur would not have leaped. Money became a way to keep score. There was nothing left that Ed could not buy which, in a way, made him less free and more dependent on using the endless sums that he was generating.

For if he could not use money in a manner that would calm his aggression, then why was he working so hard at accumulation. And if accumulation ceased to have a goal and became the goal itself, Ed sensed that he would be cheated, richly cheated but cheated nevertheless.

So one day at the Annapolis Boat show, in Henry Wagner's booth where I was signing books, this tall, spare, and elegant man introduced himself. He had known my father, which instantly endeared him to me. As a favor, he asked with appealing diffidence, would I give an opinion on a boat he wanted to buy.

I hated the boat. Ed loved it and, then and there, bought himself his first ever sailboat at the best part of a million dollars, never having so much as sailed across a lake.

Ed had no idea of the delights of sailing. He knew nothing of the blinding thrill of a landfall or the quiet self-confident delight that suffuses a sailor after a bout with a spiteful squall. Ed knew nothing of the sea save the deep conviction that this boat that he had just blindly bought would give meaning and stretch back to his life. The boat, he confessed to me later, was acquired on instinct alone. This most unpoetic man said that his heart told him to do it.

Three months later we gathered a crew and crossed

the big pond. Ed was never to be the same again. In the three weeks of passage Ed mutinied against everything he thought he held dear. In the weeks of passage he saw the shape of his future. His businesses became annoying intervals between passages. His family became crew. He limbered his no longer young muscles on the foredeck, he took his turn in the galley, he shot the sun with a sextant each day and the stars at dusk. He stowed stores, worried about the depleting tank of fresh water and, sitting cross legged on the lurching bowsprit, he mended a jib when a seam opened. These tasks, unthinkable burdens at home, became a joyous celebration of the sea.

Ed mutinied and wrought himself a sailor and, in doing so, took back his life.

THE STANDING SAILOR

One day in Rhodes I met the standing sailor. He was a Scandinavian who had run afoul of his orthopedic surgeon. Having contracted an arcane condition which necessitated a fused spinal column, he was offered a variant of Hobson's choice: either he could spend the rest of his days seated (almost unthinkable) or on his feet (almost unbearable). He chose his feet and instead of opting for the steadying reassurance of solid land which his condition certainly required, he chose to build himself a lurchabout sailboat and go to sea. A strange choice for a man who could lie down without bending only by the most extreme of calisthenic activity. But no one ever accused the standing sailor of not being strange.

The standing sailor needed, to put it mildly, special accommodations not to be had on any boatshow boat. As a result he designed and built his own, a boat both weird and wonderful and ugly which he dubbed PLATO for reasons that I never understood. It consists of a tall box (for standing up in) mounted on a pair of hulls. The box is lined with chest high shelves for eating at, and writing on, and a place to lean for naps and a bunk to throw himself into. The catamaran, for so it is, sports a rigid wing sail so much like his fused back that it could hardly have been accidental. His toilet is a slit-trench built down into one of the hulls—a particularly clever resolution of a tough problem as he managed to relieve himself standing over it.

The standing sailor is less interesting for his physical solutions than for his instinctual grasp that landlubbers would have labeled him 'invalid' if he stayed on land, while sailors, if he went to sea, would applaud his ranging spirit. The standing sailor is out there now, somewhere in the Mediterranean, potting along very slowly with his inefficient sail and less efficient back.

But he is doing it on his own, and he is free.

CHAPTER SIX

Tragic People

IN THE GREEK SENSE, tragedy is when terrible things happen to important people. The people chronicled here are, however, quite ordinary folk whose lives we touched at moments when they were losing their battles with their fates. Some won through these moments, some did not, and some neither won nor lost but continued, like Sisyphus, to bulldoze their towering rocks hopelessly up the mountain.

There is something about malevolent things that happen to sailors that is larger than life. Perhaps because it is not the stars which are the instigators of tragedy but the sailors themselves as they meet at sea a dark destiny they may well have missed otherwise.

Thomas was such a man and his tale is more poignant for his careless compulsion to put himself in harm's way. The Beggarpimps are encapsulations of all of the unimaginable ills that India forces upon its people. While not a sea tale, they were met with during our circumnavigation and represent a tragedy too large to ignore.

But I mostly cry for the man who built his chart room from dreams when he came to realize that dreams were all that remained for him.

APPOINTMENT IN PHUKET

Most of us were in Djibouti because we had had difficulties coming down the Red Sea or across the Indian Ocean. My boat was there because we had snapped a mast. The hippie trimaran, with eleven aboard, was laying over because it was falling apart after a rough passage from India. ELMO'S FIRE, 70 feet of elegant Swan, had come into collision with a freighter and was licking its wounds. Thomas and his sailboat were there for repairs after a hairy passage down the Red Sea. Neither his boat nor Thomas should have been able to make it even this far. It was evident to all of us that Thomas had stretched his luck beyond reason and should certainly venture no farther.

Thomas's boat was one of those super light, sexy, French bonbons about as heavy as celluloid and just about as strong. Any piece of flotsam bigger than a bread box was a mortal threat. It was just right for mooring (carefully, so as not to pull out the cleats) in some gold plated Mediterranean watering hole. It had no business in a harrying passage down the Red Sea. It was weightless and flimsy and extravagantly under equipped. Its owner (not Thomas, who was the skipper) had wisely opted to stay at home while his boat was being sailed to Thailand where he planned to put it out for charter. It was one of those projects where the blind abet the blind, and the lame run interference.

That Thomas made it from France was a gratuitous piece of fortune. The boat had non-operating satellite equipment and Thomas lacked a sextant and, anyway, the ability to do celestial navigation. Thomas had no experience as a skipper. His entire resume included only one passage as crew from South Africa to the Mediterranean and one passage from France to Sardinia as skipper. That he was able to talk the owner into allowing him to take the boat to Thailand is explained best by Thomas's answer to that question. "I was cheap," he said.

His crew down the Red Sea, even less experienced than he, were cowed by the experience and jumped ship and headed home to Europe, far inland to places where oars are a curiosity. But not Thomas. He had carried an inadequate boat and a landlubberly crew on his back all the rough way down to Djibouti and he would, he told me with the assurance and optimism that only a 22-year old can generate, "see it through."

That he was no skipper made him no less attractive as a person. He was bright, funny, and entertaining. His quiet compulsion to continue a passage that others would have long since abandoned was admired, albeit with sinking hearts, by those more knowledgeable than he. Luck so far. Okay. But to go forward now towards Thailand across the cantankerous Indian Ocean was spitting in the face of luck. Thomas said, "No problem. I must get to Thailand."

His telexes to the owner for repairs, funds, and new equipment went unanswered. He jury rigged as best he was able. We all helped where we could, out of concern for his safety and out of genuine affection for young Thomas.

"No matter, no matter," he would answer when we marshaled our arguments. He was proposing, we told him, to face the Indian Ocean as an inexperienced skipper, at the wrong time of the year, and in the wrong boat. It was, we complained, if not suicidal damn close to it. At least, we urged, wait a few months for better weather.

"Can't wait," said Thomas, "I have appointments in Phuket, people I must meet. Things to do. It's the beginning of the rest of my life. I'll make it. I'll make it. Stop worrying. God, you people sound like my folks. I made it this far. I'll make it."

In the face of such certainty, much of our opposition crumpled. Crumpled, that is, until we saw the crew he had rounded up.

Two boys, both younger than he. One had never even been on a sailboat before and the other was a young French derelict, whose entire experience consisted of boat sitting in harbors. But both were powerfully motivated by the police to get out of Djibouti, any old way, any way they could.

The French boy had been in trouble over drugs and was being hounded to leave. The other—the boy who had never set foot on a sailboat—was an Ethiopian refugee who had walked into Djibouti just ahead of the political horsemen of hunger and death in his country. The governments of Djibouti and Ethiopia were about to sign an agreement to return Ethiopian refugees. He would go directly from Djibouti to a slow starvation death in an Ethiopian concentration camp. He was as strongly galvanized to chance the Indian Ocean as he was ill prepared for such a passage.

With the signing of this crew we renewed our attacks on Thomas. But he, in the glory and optimism of his youth, was stronger than all of us. He would go. That was all there was to it and, because of his smile, his charm, and his insistence that his goal in Thailand must be reached, we let him go.

Inadequate Thomas with his inadequate crew in his inadequate boat hauled anchor and set sail one day. We did everything we could to help. I taught him the rudiments of the noon sight after another sailor loaned him a plastic sextant and another a very iffy old SatNav. We went over his boat pulling and tightening and strengthening. When we discovered, with horror, that he had no liferaft, we chipped in and bought a ratty old raft which still had a bit of life left in it. We prepared Thomas, his crew and his boat, as best we could for sea. It was a heartbreaking, hopeless task, but we had to do something.

Our goodbyes had a deathbed rattle. The auguries were awful. No one gave him much of a chance of making it and on the day he sailed off a dark cloak of mourning settled over the harbor. A bright and elegant light was escaping us and escaping, we were sure, life itself.

After Thomas departed the rest of us raveled up our

little cares and pressed on. I sailed back up to the Mediterranean and the others, not so impatient as Thomas, waited
for better winds in the Indian Ocean.

Months later I was at home and a postcard arrived
from Thomas in Thailand.

"Made it. Thailand is heaven. The passage not nearly
as bad as you promised. I have found meaning to my life.
I have found paradise. My thanks to you all. Thomas."

Two days later a note arrived from Inge and Rolf,
Thomas's parents in South Africa. It was a formal little
card informing us that Thomas Kinzig had been killed in
an automobile accident in Phuket shortly after his arrival.

Thomas had kept his appointment in Phuket.

DEAD THOMAS . . . A SEQUEL

When young Thomas kept his appointment in Phuket, his
appointment with death, it was reported that he had died
in a simple motor accident after miraculously surviving the
Indian Ocean at the wrong season in an inadequate boat
with an inadequate crew.

To be struck down by an unseeing fate on dry land
when all the furies of the Indian Ocean could not touch
him caused those of us who knew Thomas and loved him
to burn with a quiet anger at the injustice of the events.

That was bad enough.

But now comes worse news. Not quite news perhaps
but a story of a mother's deep knowledge of her son, and
her conviction, her certainty, that more than bad luck was
involved.

Tom's mother, Inge, is a solid, middle class, re-
spectable lady who was torn between letting Tom go to sea
and refusing to limit her young son in his puzzling (to her)
search for meaning in his life. So she let him go, filled with
forebodings that proved out in tragedy. She knew, with

that same sureness, that clouds were gathering over her beautiful young son. She knew.

When the shattering telegram arrived she was crushed, as any of us would be, but not surprised. It was too pat, too ordained, too ungodly. So she wrote to me. Since I cannot tell of the sequel with the clarity of that simple lady, who rose above her own tragedy to make her terrible story a lesson for others, I reproduce here her note, a remarkable document:

"More than eighteen months have now passed since that tragic event in Phuket and I did actually not expect to write to you again. But we have now found out something about what happened to Tom and we feel that his friends should know about it.

"We have, with the passing of these months, become more and more frustrated due to the complete lack of information regarding the events leading to his death and the fate of the yacht JOE all the more so that the owner did not see fit to contact us in any way whatsoever. I wrote letters and sent telexes to Tom's friend Mike Law in Phuket, who had arranged for the cremation and had sent us the urn. But we only received telex replies telling us that time was very scarce as he was opening his own yacht club, but that he was busy compiling a report for us. Nothing else. No report nor any of Tom's personal effects like his golden necklace, his camera, watch, photos. Nothing.

"We got more suspicious that everything was not above board when some of the details in his faxes did not tally with the police report.

"So we finally decided, for the first time in our lives, to contact a clairvoyant, the very best in South Africa, who is often employed by the police to help in murder cases and to find missing persons. It took us months to make contact with her.

"Two weeks ago my husband and I had an appointment and the first thing she said was, 'But this was murder, your son did not die in a normal accident, he was

murdered'. She said that the purpose of bringing the sailboat JOE to Thailand was, unbeknown to Tom, to use her
for drug trafficking. Once there, Thomas was asked to
participate but would not.

"He sent us a telegram for our silver wedding an-
niversary : 'Have not forgotten, am drowning in problems.
Trust me. Trust me. Love, Thomas'.

"If we had only realized what problems.

"He again had not been paid by the boat's owner or,
as he said in his last letter, he would have bought an air
ticket and surprised us at our party. The owner, the
Frenchman, knew Thomas wanted to visit us but he held
back his wages, we believe, to prevent him from leaving
Thailand.

"The clairvoyant saw three accidents before the fatal
one and Thomas had mentioned the first two. They were
meant as warnings but he ignored them and had to be silenced before he informed on the gang.

"I am telling you this for several reasons.

"Firstly, just so you know about it and to confirm
your assessment that our son was, indeed, a man of
propriety.

"Secondly, on your own voyages you might somewhere encounter JOE and maybe you might find out something, anything, more.

"Thirdly, and most importantly, that you might write
an article warning young people of the immense danger
they face in a similar situation. Anybody might be approached and not be aware of the ruthlessness of these
people. The clairvoyant said that, as clever as Thomas
was, this was big business, a syndicate, and not knowing
this he had no chance.

"Tell all the young innocents to run from these guys,
to ask help at the nearest consulate to get away from them.
And, the clairvoyant added, not to 'trust the police since
they might well be in it, too'."

That was Inge's letter. A simple appeal from a simple

lady against whom fate had struck twice. An accident was acceptable. Murder was not.

I am not a devotee of clairvoyants, but after Inge's letter arrived I reviewed my own thoughts about Thomas and about the sailboat JOE. Things just did not set right in my mind. Questions that I had buried shimmered on the surface of Inge's appeal.

When I had met JOE and Thomas in Djibouti I could not understand why a boat owner would commit such a light and underequipped craft to a skipper with no, absolutely no, ocean experience.

Why had the Frenchman refused to make any contact with Thomas in Djibouti in spite of the many telexes that Thomas had sent him?

Why had the Frenchman told Thomas that his pay depended on arriving in Thailand by a specified date although that date put JOE in the path of adverse and dangerous weather?

The story that the small, light, and inadequate JOE was being sent to Thailand for 'chartering' made no sense. Charter boats need berths, amenities, equipment, and experienced skippers and crew. JOE had none of these.

And why Thailand? There were a hundred destinations, a thousand miles closer to France, where charter would certainly have been a more probable proposition.

Thailand is, of course, where the drugs are.

Add my questions to Inge's and the inference is overwhelming that drugs lay at the core of the death of my young friend. Drugs, money, and unfeeling people who would first put a young man's life on the line against a terrible sea and then, as a convenience, kill him.

Heed the warning, young sailors, sniff out with care the folk you deal with, a touch of paranoia never hurt, and if an offer is too good to be true, well, it probably isn't.

Thomas was killed, garroted probably, or run over with a car and quickly cremated. The police, not always honest themselves, were left with only ashes to sift through.

THE BEGGARPIMPS

The scenario is painfully familiar. It is one which keeps more western tourists out of India than air fares or amoebic dysentery. It is a scenario, and it is just that, of the practiced and accomplished Indian beggar at work.

Your taxi takes you from the insulating cocoon of your hotel into the busy, lively, and ugly boulevards of Bombay. At each traffic light your cab is assaulted by limbless, crippled, mutilated beggars dumbly miming the universal cry for alms: the act of eating, of putting three fingers into their mouth, so that you are made to feel, in your own belly, their hunger.

Hungry, tearful adults are easy to ignore after a while, so the beggar culture resorts to the use of children, little children. And the impact is compounded by using little girls to lug about sleepy looking infants, as much as to say, "Look at the burden I have to carry while you taxi off to your fancy restaurants."

But the absolute worst is the use of a little girl of about three who accosts you in tatters at the curb of a busy street. As you cross the wild roadway, a dangerous act in India even for an adult, the little tyke paddles after you amid screaming tires and cursing drivers who avoid crushing her small life beneath their wheels by the narrowest of margins. Through it all she dances about you, singlemindedly pursuing you as she has been trained to do, never letting up on the cry of "No mama, no papa," while she terrorizes you (as her teachers know she will) with the danger in which she places herself. You read her unconcern at being killed in the traffic as the other side of her overwhelming hunger. Perhaps . . . but more likely it is the other side of the beating she will get if she abandons you without extracting payment for what has now become your fear, and thus your responsibility, for her very life.

Should she be killed, and it does happen, there are hordes of other three-year-olds to take her place. Should she only be crippled, then so much the better, as her twisted body becomes an exponential supplication for alms.

The poor have been with us for a very long time. None of our great religions, let alone our political inventions, have had much success in dealing with the fact that some folk end up with a lot and some with the dirty end of the stick. Some have declared the poor to be 'noble' and then allow them to suffer nobly. Others hold that the poor are somehow 'deserving', although I have never worked out whether that means that they deserve to be poor or that they deserve (but do not get) better.

In the East being poor is thought of as paying for your evil doings in your previous incarnation, but this is complicated by the proposition that holy men must abjure all material things. Poverty in the East is next to godliness. Poverty is therefore viewed as either payment for the sins of your past lives, for which you should be pitied, or a sign of the most extreme holiness, for which you must be honored. Both pity and honor require the gift of offerings.

In India there are four ways for the poor to approach their poverty. He or she might steal. He may die, which he usually does sooner than most. She may become a prostitute at the age of eight or, failing all else, become a beggar.

Begging is much to be preferred over prostitution if only because it represents a longer career opportunity. Beggars go on and on, and improve as they get older, while Indian prostitutes are has-beens at the age of fourteen. Prostitutes quickly become occupationally and terminally diseased, while beggars are subject to only the usual, not venereal, pandemics of that petri dish country. And begging pays much, much better.

It is very hard to get rich in India by peddling your ass, especially since most of the pittance goes to the pimps and the police. What little is left goes to the landlord of the father of the prostitute to pay off his debts. Better, far better, to become a beggar.

In the big cities of India, Bombay, Calcutta, Delhi, the street beggar is as much a part of the scenery as is sleeping on the sidewalk and death in the gutter. On the streets of these great cities people do indeed beg, sleep, and die at your feet but this does not make these remarkable cities any the less great. In other cultures these agonies are neatly hidden. India lets it all hang out.

The royal road to beggardom is not all peaches and cream. In fact an Indian beggar may very well have inherited his high calling from a beggar father or beggar mother or, failing that, he must achieve his art and profession by indenturing himself to one of the beggarpimps.

It is no accident that the best street corners are manned by the most piteous of creatures. Nor is it an accident that the same beggar occupies the same location day in, day out and at the very best spots, night in and night out. One would think that there would be a turnover, or at the very least a destitution of beggars, all vying with each other for your alms, at each location. No accident indeed, as all of the action is orchestrated, even down to the training of new recruits, by the lordly and very rich beggarpimps.

The beggarpimps of India control all the begging in that country with the possible exception of a few of the truly holy men. The holy men do not beg as we know it. They have no material possessions other than a cloth to cover their bodies on a chilly night and a tin plate into which offerings, mostly of food, seldom of money, are placed. There is no supplication, no asking, no gestures of hunger, no whining and, best of all, no acknowledgment of a gift once given. The gifts to the holy men are to their Lord (and yours) and are anyway in the interest of your own salvation, so any 'thank you' from the recipient would be redundant and in bad taste.

The holy men account for only the slightest part of the take of begging. The beggarpimps pull in the major part with the efficiency of a slot machine in Atlantic City stripping a little old lady from Hackensack of her rent money. The beggarpimps represent a serious industry and an impressive cash flow. But they do have expenses and problems peculiar to their industry.

A beggarpimp must have, first and foremost, his locations. He must own or be able to control those corners where he places his beggars. He must be strong enough to fight off, physically if necessary, the raids of other lesser pimps. This being India physical force is rarely needed. So the successful beggarpimp must be rich enough to buy the police with their whole ascending order of official outstretched palms. He lets his employees, the police, take care of his less rich competition. (Since the policeman's salary is less than is necessary to even barely sustain life, graft is built into the needs of the community for police protection. It's a kind of taxation which cannot be evaded as easily as are most official forms of Indian taxation.)

Next the beggarpimp needs beggars. And since the average Indian is long inured to suffering, either real or fictional, the beggars must be of such a terrible condition that they will attract the jaded attention of the upper castes. This is pretty difficult to do since, from sheer self-protection, the upper class Indians simply do not see even the real suffering about them. They can pick their way through a street of coughing, dying children and truly not even remember having done so.

As a result the successful beggar must reach an ever higher plateau of horror to attract the attention of the tunnel-visioned passerby. The problem that the beggarpimp faces is that nature only provides so many human horrors and those she does produce are rarely as bad as is required to stop traffic.

So the beggarpimp takes matters into his own creative hands and, using infants in the same manner that a sculpture uses clay, produces human objects guaranteed to assure him his cash flow. The usual expedient of lopping off arms or legs, or the more effective method of deforming limbs in infancy into phantasmagoria of the human forms, carries with it the inefficiency of needing to provide assistance to the beggar for the things that he cannot now do for himself. As a result there has grown a school of horrormakers which holds that deformity must not interfere with function. Make the beggar look awful but leave him with the ability to get about and look after himself. It's cheaper, they argue.

As a result, and because the beggarpimps are subtle students of behavioral psychology, the emphasis is turning to facial deformation. When we look at someone we are conditioned to look into their face and if the horror lies there, maximum and numbing impact is instantly achieved.

Any embryologist could immediately separate 'normal' deformations that can happen to the human body from those that simply cannot happen in the womb. Since we are all not embryologists, when you are confronted with a child whose upper gum and lips were tied in infancy with cords to create the most grotesque effects, your heart is torn and your pocketbook is opened. And thus you become personally responsible for the next screaming infant who is so tortured, just as if you tied the binding thongs with your own hands.

The beggarpimps get rich and the beggars . . .Well at least they get fed, but not too well, mind you, for what possible use is a fat beggar. The little three-year-old girls who are not killed or maimed in the traffic are sold (for they are owned by the beggarpimps) into prostitution and those too old or too ugly for the brothels are afforded the opportunity to die, unattended, in the streets.

So, my friends, do not give to Indian beggars no matter how heartrending the prospect. Should you do so, the sin of their agony may stain your own soul and cause you to return in your next incarnation as a rat or a cockroach, or even, God forbid, as an Indian beggar in the hands of a beggarpimp.

THE CHART ROOM

A man I knew died not long ago. He was a star crossed man who started life well and, for no discernible, cosmic reason, was obliged to end it early.

I knew him first in high school where he was the best dresser, the best dancer, and the most sought after catch by all the girls at school. He was a natural leader who did not require that touch of machismo which, in those innocent days, was for most a prerequisite for leadership. He was slim, likeable, quiet and had a perfect understanding of the extent and the limits of the adolescent world which he shaped and to which he responded.

He was effortless in his academics and where he faltered a bit his natural charm hoisted him that extra grade denied to those less gracious. He was, of course, president of his class in his senior year and editor of the class yearbook. He was the "man most likely to . . ."

The college he chose was ivy walled and the fraternities pledged him first among the incoming freshmen. His college career was a four-year, satisfying repeat of his high school achievements.

He graduated respectably and married his high school sweetheart, by far the prettiest girl the school had ever produced. He moved to Chicago and started a business career amidst the ease and grace of adoring families, both his own and his in-laws. He was successful from the start.

Then his enemy surfaced for the first time. Some called it God, some called it the devil, and some called it genes.

His doctor called it diabetes. The disease was fought desperately throughout his shortened life. Diets and injections and then, finally, amputations were harbingers of the end toward which he was rushing. He died a young man.

I had pursued my own career less gracefully than he. In the end I gravitated toward the sea. I had just published a book on the sea and I found myself in Chicago promoting the book on a local radio station. The beautiful lady who had been his wife heard me and called my hotel. She had, she said, something to show me. Something in which I would be interested. Would I please make the time to come out to the house in the suburbs where they had lived since coming to Chicago?

At her home I was led to a locked door on which the curious legend "No hard shoes please" was tacked. Upon entering I glanced about and found myself in my own world.

When my dead friend recognized, early in his short life, that he would never have the broad access to the world that his radiant youth had promised, he created, in this room where I now stood, a *Chart Room*, as he called it. It was his private world of sea passages. Here were the travels of the great sailors, which he had culled from the literature of the sea. It was not enough for my friend to plot their passages on the charts which lined the walls of the room. Each voyage had been logged as if he himself had been skipper, as if he himself had sailed them. He had built an imaginary world for himself from which, he already well knew, he would never emerge.

I came away from that room in Chicago with a clearer understanding of my own need to shed the land, my drive to get out to sea. Even though my friend never made it himself, he had created an effective device to break the grip of the illness that locked him to the land. He had triumphed over his enemy. In the end he was far freer than most of us.

Those of us who are able to go from imaginary voyages to the real oceans might well build our own chart rooms. These rooms, if we are lucky, are 'open sesames' to a life of freedom at sea. Should malign events intervene that are beyond our powers to counteract, we can at least have our dreams.

The chart room is much more than that familiar image of the armchair sailor dreaming of far shores. It demands work and dedication. It requires that there is gathered together in one place all of the stuff of which passages are made. It allows us to log passages in their entirety from concept to completion and thus get a feel of the sea so that when we finally cast off our real dock lines, all we need do is recall a chart room passage. The real passage will be easy since we have already made it once in our mind.

The chart room is our first resource and our first step toward the passages we will someday make. In our chart room we will twist our dream into the beginning of tangible reality. In it we are introduced to the charts, the literature, the technical publications, and the endless averages of ocean sailing. These materials of passage flesh out our dreams in print and bring into the sunshine of possibilities the moonshine inside our heads.

Constrained in the small space of a chart room, locked tight to the land, we can escape geography and time and conjure up the vast oceans and the small boats that will carry us across them.

AN UNEARNED DEPRESSION

An old sailor friend dropped by the other day. It was a pleasant surprise, as we had not seen him for months. He had become, his young wife had reported, depressed and nastily argumentative. In self-defense she had temporarily moved off the boat and was considering worse.

René, as we shall dub him, arrived in a convertible BMW, one of three nice cars in the family that served his two homes besides his boat. Being French, he was dressed as usual in his nattiest, cutest, most nautical best. He had always been a nifty dresser and, depressed or no, he had not lost the knack.

René is 74 and has behind him a distinguished Washington-based career in high level hospitality. He has a nice nest egg, not huge but better than most, two houses, a charming wife who earns a considerable salary, a passel of rich friends in Paris who gladly pay his way when he visits as he has done this past year for three months. In addition, he has a blue water boat in which he has not quite completed a circumnavigation. Except for the fact that he is not thirty, René seems to have little to regret and damn all about which to be depressed.

When I asked him how he was and he replied "good," I knew that something was amiss. René always talks in extravagances. The theater, films, ocean passages, people he has met and other matters are either " 'orrible" or "utterly fantastically wonderful." Just "good" signaled that my friend René was up to his Gallic ears in *merde*.

He finally admitted to a depression which he blamed at first on his age. He quoted a French actress who at 80 described old age as "disgusting."

After much discussion, René, rheumy eyed, confessed that it was not that he was old that affected him but that "being old was inelegant." He could not, vain as he is, abide the thought that he was losing his considerable, youthful beauty. He pulled up his shirt to disclose a taut, flat belly, and then complained that his legs were the basis of his depression.

"When I climb the stairs I must hold the rail for fear of falling. It is 'orrible, I must be nearing my end." It came clear that his end was not near when he announced that his mother's 100th birthday was in the works.

René is a tangled nest of contradictions. With marvelous genes he will reach a century. Free of basic financial worries he can afford the month in Bali for which he yearns. Married to a sexy and beautiful woman he dreams of Balinese girls. The world has denied him little and yet, out of pure hubristic vanity, he claws his way down into a dangerous emotional pit.

"Most men live lives of quiet desperation," but the only desperation with which René must contend is that he is no longer as youthfully elegant as he once was.

There is a lesson there. He lives in an age that has chemically banished pain and offers him decades more of high quality life. His heart can be replaced if needed. René can use simple pills for illnesses that only a few decades ago would have killed him off. His government takes care of astronomical hospital costs and now with Prozac and Viagra the two core causes of elderly distress are remissionable.

Considering all of the above and his own fortunate circumstances, René has little pretext for resentment and depression. And yet he was able to root about in his ego until he managed to distress the folk who love and respect him.

The human animal is so astoundingly intellectually adept that where cause does not exits, it invents cause. Man's ability to invent can lead away from greatness as easily as it can toss out a Shakespeare or define parsecs-broad regions of an unseeable universe.

Most causes of depression have been scientifically and socially elided for us ancients at the beginning of the twenty-first century. We are blessed and, should we reject these blessings, we commit a foolishness beyond measure.

And yet, even in our animosity at the Renés of this world, do we not all have those days when the dark mantle settle for no discernible reason? In those somber hours we can empathize with those sufferers of unearned depressions even as we fight to regain the perspective by which we carry on living.

We are, after all, our brothers and we must look after ourselves.

CHAPTER SEVEN

Incredible People

HERE ARE SOME REALLY incredible people. They grace these chronicles as folk who, through either their actions or their characters, overleap what we ordinary folk may even dream of.

Creamer earned his place for a voyage unlike any of the past and which can never be surpassed in the future. From whence he summoned up the pure arrogance even to undertake such a passage remains a mystery, one of those mysteries that makes the rest of us tingle with pleasure for the human spirit.

Kung is here because he epitomized mystery and stamped each of us who knew him with his ineradicable brand.

And Tristan, well, because he was Tristan. Because he, from among all of the folk I have ever known or perhaps ever could know, shouted defiance in the face of the gods, and almost got away with it.

CREAMER DOES WITHOUT (MULTUM IN PARVO)

It is here argued that recent technological advances in sailing the deep oceans are dangerous, because of their potential for failure and, what is possibly more important, they have taken the fun out of passaging great distances in a small boat.

When you know that you can do without this or that pulsating, electronic sorcerer, you can go to sea with more ease. When the bleeps go belly up you can get down to the ancient business of divining a course from here to there with little more than the miracles of your mind and eyes. You become an ancient mariner using ancient techniques.

I carry a compass, a sextant, an RDF, a GPS, a knot log, a radio and a quartz watch, all of which were invented within the last 200 years. People have been sailing for so much longer, perhaps 10,000 years, that my caution in equipment is belt and suspenders stuff.

Suppose I were to attempt a circumnavigation *sans* sextant, *sans* radio, *sans* instruments, and without even a watch. Crazy, you say. Sure, but someone crazier than I did just that.

A few years ago, Marv Creamer, a high school geography teacher with little experience of the sea, set sail with nothing, save his own mind and eyes. No radio, no GPS, no instruments, no compass, not even a watch. Yet, he completed this barest bones world circumnavigation safely and elegantly in seventeen months.

It is a feat of which I will forever be jealous. It was the truly impossible voyage. It was a recapitulation of what sailors did millennia ago even before they were convinced that they would not fall off the edge of the world.

In the light of Marv Creamer's epic, what we did in UNLIKELY is kid's stuff. Creamer taught us that in the final analysis we are smarter than our machines, a fact that often escapes us when we peer into the bottomless electronic data pits that direct our lives. But pits they are, great puddles of undisciplined information that await the application of our miracle brains to make sense.

Marv Creamer solved the electronic pit problem by banishing them entirely from his passage and going directly to the source of all understanding: his naked brain, the stars above him, and the setting and rising sun.

His achievement passed quietly. A few acknowledgements in the sailing press and an article or two in his hometown paper. The larger implications were missed in the welter and fog of news that engulfs us.

This Luddite of the sea offered all of us who sail the opportunity to take back from modern navigational devices some of the self-confidence they have stolen from us.

I hope we are listening.

THE MANY FACES OF DR. KUNG

Gray beard trimmed to extinction, feet shod in sandals crafted by small hands in the East, dressed in Thai silk pants full in the stern like a third leg and draped loosely to the waist into which was tucked a matching shirt, he wafted about the lobby of the Pera Palas in Istanbul, perfectly at home. It was the hotel and the city that seemed displaced.

His image, not diminished by a slender bamboo stick too light and too long for walking, evoked the other worldly wisdoms of a Japanese *Go* master or a Korean elder deeply versed in the way of tea. But Kung was neither Japanese nor Korean. He had too few syllables for the former and too flat a face for the latter. Kung was an Inner Mongolian, born far from the western shadow of the Great Wall.

Consequence and cachet enrobed him like the floating

veils of Salome. Dignity and restraint washed up on those he passed and, *en passant*, unraveled small cares of living. After only a glance all yearned to know him. He cast about him a sense of truth, a reserve of ultimate meanings. He was the master whom you had pursued since the terrible day you lost your innocence.

If Kung said life was a fountain then life was a fountain . . . Like everyone else at the Pera Palas I was in his thrall. I itched to meet him, to learn from him. I suddenly knew why I had come to Istanbul. Not to photograph the legendary Pera Palas as I had thought, but to cross the path of Kung. Truth revealed was just around the corner.

But how was I to approach such reserve? How to intrude on the large thoughts with which Kung must be dealing even as he wandered the lobby greeting groups and delegations who, fortunate persons, had audience with him? My eye fell upon my forgotten cameras. I would wait until he settled somewhere and set up as if to photograph the area. Then I would contrive, somehow, anyhow, to meet him.

After dispersing various respectful petitioners about the room, Kung settled at the head of a table around which a small group were gathered. I took a deep breath and tossed caution, and my life, to the winds of chance. "Could I please," I faltered, "photograph your group to add a bit of life to the lobby?" Even to my own ear I sounded like a groupie after a rock star autograph.

At my request Kung rose, almost apologetically, from his seat. Directly addressed, he backed off as if the volume of the confrontation was turned a bit too high. He receded then stepped forward in a timorous, birdlike approach-avoidance dance that made you feel, acutely, the barbarian that you were. His answers, to any question or statement, were in whispered, stretched out phrases, as if each thought and each word must be weighed for truth and import before release.

"Yes? Well," pause, pause, "ah perhaps," pause, step back, "someone more," step forward, very long pause, "ah, acceptable than me?"

I felt I had just crushed a violet.

"No, no," I begged. "Please, it will only take a moment."

Kung dipped his head, smiled like a sunrise, swept the lobby as if looking for just the exactly correct response to make to this impertinence, yet not wanting to suggest affront, sighed and whispered.

"Oh . . . yes, yes. It will," pause, a dance step back, a dance step forward, "perhaps, be fine. I will be, may be, should be . . . pleased . . ." His voice trailed off and he wandered distractedly away. I did not know what to make of his departure, but he soon wandered back, looked surprised to see me, and breathed,"Ah, yes. The photograph. Of course . . . it will," pause, as if seeking amiable escape. Then a deep breath of resigned acquiescence, "Yes, oh yes. I am honored. Will this table," he cast about for the word, "befit?"

My spirit soared. I had been granted my boon. I had heard the voice of the turtle and it spoke to me.

Taking a very long time, I took my photograph, had a few words with Kung, and wished for more. But with an uncharacteristic rush of modesty, brought on by Kung's vaulting dignity and reticence, I abandoned him, with painful reluctance, to his ever increasing flock.

Later that morning, as I dawdled over a cup of coffee and rubbed softly against the memory of my moment with Kung, he wandered of his own volition to my table and asked, over his shoulder as he passed, a very curious question.

"I am told," a distant look, a long sigh, "but perhaps I am wrong? Sorry," as he turned away.

"No, no. What? What?" My voice was rising in uncontrollable falsetto as I sought to hold him for yet one more precious moment.

"Ah, yes . . . that you are . . . huh . . . that you have a sailing vessel. Is that true? To what destination do you go?"

I finally had him on my own conversational ground.

"West, toward Greece."

"And . . . but perhaps I should not ask . . . well," long pause, "how many individuals do you sail with on your boat?"

"Four: my wife, my brother, a cousin, and myself," I answered, wanting to tell him so much more.

"And," he asked as he danced lightly toward and away from me, his voice, a mere whisper, rising and falling with the distance, "how many more persons could your boat accommodate?"

A very curious question. But from Kung one came quickly to expect the curious. And an even more stunning follow up.

"Perhaps," the longest pause yet, almost as if the conversation were over, "perhaps, uh, huh, yes . . . perhaps I shall accompany you for a day or two."

My voice failed and all I could do is nod with such vigor that my glasses slid down my nose. Finally, even falsetto failing me, I croaked,

"Oh, yes. You would be so welcome. It would be an honor, an honor." I wanted to kiss his sandalled feet.

"Yes, it might be . . . "pause, pause, shuffle and smile and a short walk away then back, "nice. We shall see . . . won't we?" His smile crinkled his eyes behind his Ben Franklin glasses.

He could have had my first born and all he wanted was all I wanted, to be together, close and intimate. For some hours to take from him a bit of his quiet, his other-worldliness, his contentment. To have him with me on my boat was, perhaps, the reason why I owned the boat at all.

Kung drifted away, his feet barely touching the floor. Mine did not at all.

The rest of the afternoon was filled with the small

blips of exaltation that come when you know that the world is okay and so are you. I sat and drank frothy cold coffee, *frappé* they call it in Turkey, that was one part coffee and ten parts sugar. Diet? To hell with diet. All is stress anyway and I was to be totally unstressed by Kung. To what extent, however, I could not have imagined.

Kung continued to hold court. A moment here, a nod or word there, was all that was needed to keep large groups of active and important looking people content just to be. I could not envision what Kung was accomplishing. Perhaps just making their lives a little better?

At tea time a lady walked into the lobby and paused at the head of the stairs. She was distinguished without being at all beautiful, important without a strong presence, and, in her black-and-white checkered dress, rather more of her existed than she might have preferred.

There are moments in the theater when on a busy stage all lights fade save those on selected protagonists. All activity in the play seems to cease, except for the words and movements, now dreamlike in their isolation, of the players left lonesome in the spotlights.

Just so, at that moment in the lobby of the Pera Palas, the entire room dimmed and all eyes and lights turned on the arresting woman and Kung.

At the moment she appeared, Kung had his back to the entrance. He had been listening intently to the woes of a small group of Americans who had passaged humbly to see him in far Istanbul from an exalted institution on the Hudson River. As the lady entered behind him, I watched Kung's back stiffen and come to sharp attention. He wheeled about, faster than any motion he had made all day and, trailing his dignity in a turbulent wake, hurried, no, scampered, toward the lady. In his eagerness his head reached far out in front of his feet converting, in an instant, this reposeful sage into a cartoony Road Runner.

He skidded up to her, took both her hands and cried,

"My God! What did you do to yourself? You're thin, you're beautiful. You have lost a hundred pounds!"

With the shy, proud, smile of the formerly fat, the lady said, "Oh, perhaps a hundred grams."

"My God, the Dragon Lady! Come, run away with me, tell the ambassador you have a better offer. Come, Dragon Lady, now!"

The ambassador's wife, for so she proved to be, bathed in Kung's delight. He, so excited that he could not contain himself, suddenly leapt straight up into the air in front of her and then leapt again and again, bouncing like a small African antelope springing its height in exuberance. I have never seen such approbation, such reinforcement, such benediction.

Kung and the lady, now easily ten years younger, disappeared in the direction of the bar, with Kung still popping into the air beside her as he continued to urge and coax her to defect with him.

What had happened to my gentle master? Where was the repose, the shyness, the delicious hesitancy? What had happened to Kung? Whom would I be sailing with tomorrow?

That evening Kung, when I refused to accept payment, took us out to dinner. With relief I found the old Kung, the first Kung, deftly and quietly hosting the meal.

The episode with the ambassador's wife faded, perhaps never had happened. But an insight into his passionate depths remained and confused and bemused any attempt to get a firm handle on Kung.

Kung talked of sailing. He had never sailed and apologized, painfully, for imposing himself upon us. His auto-invitation, he explained, was part of his search for knowledge and experience. He had, he told us, listened to many sailors and had often wondered what the charm of the sea could be. Our appearance was a serendipitous

(Kung actually used the word) event, a gift from the gods. The early shyness, the hesitancy, the approach-avoidance, his pleasing sensation of unsureness of self spread out again and covered us with a warming quilt of good feeling and endless approval.

The dinner became a game of "Who Is Kung?" We had determined, from his exquisitely designed calling card, that he held a visiting professorship at the University of the Bosphorus. The card, not quite the right size and subtly rounded at the corners, also indicated that his residence was the Pera Palas Hotel. A visiting professor? Domiciled at the most expensive *caravanserai* in Istanbul? Everything we learned led from mystery to mystery and Kung, born to the eastern arts of misdirection, allowed no easy insights.

Although he never actually defined it, his field seemed to be cultural anthropology. One of the calling cards he passed to us—we were becoming aware of his many hats—identified Kung as a professor at the prestigious and tradition laden University of Kyoto. For a non-Japanese to be so honored was most unusual. For the foreigner to be Mongolian, a culture both despised and adulated at the same time (and thus twice rejected) by the Japanese, was unheard of. Kung gave us only the bare facts. He did hold such a chair. He had left it for a position at the University of the Bosphorus, an institution that grazed in only the bare and distant verges of cultural anthropology. Why had he left such centrality for such a bushland? We should have known better than to ask Kung so direct a question. But an answer of sorts did come out later.

Two other appointments which he had held, and which he reluctantly described to us, pointed toward intellectual adventurism that contradicted his meek and accepting image.

"For a while," he murmured," I was the cultural advisor to the king of Nepal." Then, with his usual inability to pass straightforward information (of which there seemed not to be any in his universe) he added the word, "ostensibly." What he did with the king, except to meet with him once a week, never came out and how does one function as an 'ostensible' advisor?

Even more beguiling was his part time appointment with the Hallmark Card company. Added to that vast cornucopia of homily, Kung held an appointment that he had dubbed "cross-cultural advisor." It seemed, he explained, that Hallmark, recognizing the enormous sense of social insufficiency (Kung's term) that runs through Japanese life, decided that Japan was a promising market for easy sentiment. But an idiom was needed and the translation of 'roses are red and violets are blue' to parseable Japanese was accomplished with Kung's embarrassed and exquisite assistance.

"But they did pay extremely well," he recalled with some wistfulness. Aha, we thought, another Kung, a mercenary, unamateur Kung, emerges.

The meal finished, we said goodnight. Kung, hands steepled in front of him, bowed deeply to each of us in turn and wandered off. To the ambassador's wife? My mostly gentle, studiedly moral, ascetic appearing Kung? Banish the titillating thought!

The next morning, in company with a forlorn, about to be bereft retinue, Kung appeared at the dock. Thirty people saw him off, many in tears. The ambassador's wife, standing quietly behind the crowd, looked proud.

Kung offered a papal blessing to the abandoned ones and stepped aboard. His sense of how to act on a sailboat was intuitively correct. His luggage was small and soft. His sandals came off before his feet touched the deck. He failed to wrench at the Loran antenna at the stern as he mounted the rail. He touched no line as he came aboard and, once on deck, he magically reduced himself in size by half and for the rest of the voyage never once was in anyone's way.

Had he never really been sailing before? Kung assured us that he had not. Kung had raised to a high level the East's ability to conform to circumstances. He had an innate, fine tuned sense of propriety—when he so chose.

Kung had arranged for us to decide, contrary to our original intention and without our conscious volition, that we sail to the small Turkish port of Çanakkale. Kung hinted that it would be immoral to pass up Schliemann's excavations at Troy which lay only an hour or so inland from Çanakkale and, additionally, he wanted to make us a special gift, a thank you for the passage, by bringing us to the tiny fishing village of Assos. "Two restaurants, no hotels, and approachable only by sea, by four wheel drive vehicles or by any German tourist driving anything," Kung explained with a sly smile.

During the two days of the passage from Istanbul, Kung, already a wraith, became less and less substantial. Like the Cheshire cat, at times he seemed little more than a smile as he let himself sink into the spirit and texture of passing over a sea in a sailing vessel. The pace and tempo, the speed, or lack of it, intensified Kung's essentially meditative personality. There is no memory of his having eaten and certainly no memory of any organized sleep. From time to time he would be found napping, stretched out on the foredeck, belly and smile to the sky, his mouth tensionless and slightly ajar. He seemed, for these few hours, to be shedding, forever, the last thin threads of connection to corporeal life. We delighted in providing the agency for his distancing but we feared that an even more unsubstantial Kung might vanish altogether, leaving us as bereft as the stricken wavers at the dock in Istanbul. Or so we thought.

When he could be urged to talk, Kung's insights ran intellectual chills up the spine. He described the Japanese as a "bonzai culture," small, neat, controlled, disciplined and formed by the perpetual resourceless poverty of Japan. Not having much they made big out of little. Being used to little and small, they were the masters of, among other small things, the semi conductor, "a bonzai device if there ever was one."

He shared, with the rest of the Orient, a mainland disdain for the Japanese. Korea, Mongolia, and China peer down on the nervous little isles to the east from their own historical and cultural Himalayas. He came, he explained with surprising immodesty, from a society that was already millenia old before the Japanese even began to imitate it. Would he be returning to Japan, we asked?

"No . . . I think not. No." Kung paused and allowed himself a little review, you could see it writ in his eyes. "No. I cannot imagine that I would so . . . limit myself . . . ever again." Here was the exegesis of his withdrawal from the kudos of Kyoto.

He had, it transpired, lived in America, studied and taught at the University of Southern California, and surprise! surprise! he was an American citizen. He complained that he had "wasted America." He should have sucked more experience out of its vast and rich culture during the time he was there. "I was too taken with its riches to pause and learn," he sighed with the regret of the student who recognizes too late how much there is to know. "It is an experience that overcomes many new immigrants to America. I had come into heaven . . . so why not enjoy?"

A 'wasted America' was a new idea. Kung came back to the theme again and again.

"People speak of wasting their lives, wasting opportunities. I wasted an entire continent, an entire history, an entire culture. I shall never be able to regain the unique, open-eyed wonder of those first few months. I submerged myself in a warm and voluptuous bath filled with pleasant, soapy bubbles."

With painful embarassment he ventured a peculiar plaint: "This passage . . . it is perhaps too pleasant. As it was in America the winds are mild and the sun is clear and the air is pure. It is, a thousand, thousand pardons . . . it could be, perhaps, just a bit grittier?"

We explained that things on a sailing passage were often worse to the point of incapacitation. Kung liked that word. "Incapacitation as a way to truth? Yes, that is very eastern. Perhaps you sailors lean closer to Zen than you might like to admit." He smiled quietly and then said, "Thank you. I have learned something about sailing. I have learned something about the West. I have filled in a small American gap."

When we pressed him to share his discovery with us he said, "A teacher urges, never directs, hints, never explains, asks questions, never gives answers. Patience, patience."

It was on notes like these, scarce on most sailboats, that we passed a day and two nights of a quiet passage. All previous interpersonal tensions of the crew disappeared in the soothe of Kung's quiet delight in the sea. He reminded us, sailors whose first tastes of the sea were decades old and whose sense of wonder was a bit dulled in time, of the jubilate moments of our own first passages. He required us to smell, to look, to hear, and to feel the sea as a new experience. Most tyros aboard a sailboat require teaching. This tyro taught.

Then as we pulled into Çanakkale, the great 'Kungian transition' occurred. At first it seemed a mild request, perfectly fitting the gentle and appreciative Kung we had come to know.

"Please, captain, for two days I have enjoyed a great gift from you. I have come to know some of the delights of allowing oneself to just be aboard a small boat in a very large sea. I gave myself up to the sea, to the boat, to an experience that I could hardly have had without you. For two days I centered myself as I rarely ever could on land. I can thank you for letting me serve under you at sea only by requesting, respectfully," he receded a bit and came forward, the old Kung backing and filling, "that you allow me, in name only of course, to be the captain of our next few hours on land. I have my wonders to share with you as you shared the wonders of the sea with me. With your permission, and I apologize for even asking, I want, for just these few hours, to be your obedient master. Please."

An obedient master? We should have smelled a Mongolian rat. But to serve at his feet was all we had ever desired. We granted his request, giggling like children as we did so.

At this the transition, complete and total, occurred. Kung leaped straight up into the air, spun about sandalled feet churning, and landed running toward a green minibus that had been parked on the quay at a not too discreet distance. Could Kung have orchestrated his intentions in advance? Without first obtaining our acquiescence? You bet he could.

As he ran he trailed his voice after him, loud and twice life size. "Hurry, hurry! We have not a moment to lose. Schliemann awaits. Assos awaits, the ancients await. Come. Now! Hurry, our chariot," he swept an arm toward the suspect green mini, "awaits."

Kung was bounding with excitement. The reserve and modesty had been washed away in the pleasure of sharing some of his world with us. He was plumbing the delights of violent activity. He shed, in a nanosecond, the centered reserve and threw himself outward in all directions at once. Where were his cautions of urges and hints? Kung was directing, ordering, leaping over the battlements yards ahead of his panting, stunned troops. Gone, utterly gone, was even a faint whiff of the effacing East. He was Alexander astride a great white charger towing a resistant, dazed, and groggy army in his wake.

We were hungry, we complained, as we puffed up to the van and suggested that perhaps we should stop for a snack. We should have known better.

"Never mind, never mind. All aboard. We will eat on the way. I will provide everything. Get in, get in!"

We were shoved aboard, helter-skelter, like Japanese commuters on the Tokyo subway, falling over each other in his haste. Barely had he slammed the door, narrowly avoiding a small amputation, that he scampered, silks aflutter, around to the front, leapt in, slammed his door and screeched, "*Avanti, avanti*" to his open-mouthed, uncomprehending Turkish driver who thought, he told us later, "that I had been hired by this nice, gentle oriental gentleman who suddenly became a whirling dervish."

No sooner had he ordered us forward than he yelled at the driver to stop. Without explanation, he leapt from the skidding, halting van and disappeared. After a few puzzled moments we went in search of our 'gentle master'. We found him in a small restaurant which he had reduced, in his frenzy to be off to Troy, to catatonic shock. He had amassed, in minutes, a pile of food enough to last us for days and was demanding cases of beer. "Cold, cold beer," he shouted, "my friends like their beer cold, ice cold!" In a small village in a country where cold beer was a curiosity, Kung, by force of personality alone, materialized a case of cold beer. He tossed uncounted bills to the stunned proprietor and with whoops of victory, the beer held aloft like a conqueror's flag, he danced us back to the van leaving the restaurateur without food, exhausted, abstracted and wondering from what strange and unknown land had appeared the small yellow typhoon.

The ride to Troy was full of cries of consummate, physical glee of being alive and doing exactly what felt right. Nothing more. Nothing less. Kung forced us to eat more than we wanted, to drink more than we thought we could. Restraint, the costume in which we had first met Kung, was replaced by undiluted excess. Immoderation in all things, especially in moderation, was part of Kung's many faces.

Suddenly, along the winding country lane that leads into the valley of Priam and Helen, of Achilles and Odysseus, Kung screamed again for the driver to stop. The driver, reacting now to any order from Kung, screeched to a stop at the extreme brink of a hundred-foot drop. Balancing at full bore along the verge Kung was out the door and racing back toward a small, venerable and thoroughly startled Turk astride an even smaller and equally venerable donkey.

"My dream, my dream! It is my dream come true!" Kung raced toward the mounted ancient Turk who was by this time frantically urging his donkey up the hill and away from the wild incubus who had thrust himself into his old man's reverie.

"This is my dream. Me and a donkey. That's all. That's all. Shed of all I own, honors, name and position, with only a scrap of clothing and my small donkey, my small and lovely donkey. To thus wander the world, shorn of wealth, naked and necessitous. To find Truth. It is the only way. It is the way of the old man and his donkey."

The old man and his donkey. Kung the penurious wanderer. Another Kung. Less of a surprise than others. We were becoming accustomed to his faces.

There is no end to this tale. No denouement wherein the real Kung emerges. There is no real Kung. He is all men, everyman, pro and con, thesis and antithesis, questions and answers, without the merest suggestion of embarrassing contradiction.

His gifts to us were acceptance and joy. Inordinateness, indulgence, discipline, restraint and excess. And especially approbation, total approval of whatever we were. For whatever we yearned to be, Kung stood on the side lines, countenancing and validating, sometimes with a small and delicate gesture of encouragement and sometimes with the "go, man, go!" of a football coach. Whatever felt right for him at the moment. His shifts from face to face, from image to image, were his acknowledgement of all experiences, his permission for us to be whatever we chose.

Kung gave us Troy. He summoned it up out of Homer and wandered with us through the true myths of our pasts. Then he bundled us, awhooping and awailing aboard his 'green chariot' and prodded the driver into screeching turns and precipitous drops down to the tiny, touristless fishing village of Assos. As we sped over the last hill and looked down the Agean, calmed by distance and blued by a cloudless sky, Kung greeted the water and announced with a touch of longing,

"We shall take off all our clothes, admire our bodies and skinny dip in ancient seas. And perhaps we shall make love."

Another Kung.

TALES OF TRISTAN

Those of us who sail and dream and find that our dreams are just an approximation of reality reveled in the adventures of Tristan in which fantasy overleaped fact. In his books he let us join him in impossible adventures, just those adventures that we would wish for ourselves, and who cared what the balance was between fact and fiction.

That he sailed in the most difficult climes is fact. His confrontations and battles with petty officials were fact. How he bested them, how he turned impossible odds to great victories are neither fact nor fiction. Tristan's battles against the odds, as he described over and over in his books, were little more than his irascible railing against the larger officialdom of fate.

I have two tales to tell of Tristan. Without his talent to swell small events into large confrontations they will be less interesting than he would have made them. But they are true and, even uninflated, they give the flavor of the man.

There came a time when I innocently sought to convert an ancient little harbor built by Constantine on the Black Sea into a modern Romanian marina. The project was beset by pettiness and obstacles, which process is brought to a high art by the Romanians. In trying to deal with this I came to believe that only a Tristan Jones could smash through the barriers daily set upon us.

I asked him to come to Romania and be the commodore of the Constanta Yacht Club and the captain of the port. His job, which he accepted with an evil, joyous glint in his eye, was to whip these recalcitrant folk into shape.

He failed. But for a most curious reason.

He stormed into Romania on his one good leg and set about as only he could to make a silk purse. He spent the worst winter of his life in that small harbor roaring up and down the docks in his wheelchair, spreading panic and terror. In the spring he confessed to me that, in spite of towering rages and brutal tantrums, the battle was lost. Since I had seen him through worse times I was curious to know how he had failed to conquer mere men when he had so often and so handily conquered the gods themselves.

"I'll tell you, boyo. The gods were easy. They stood and fought. The Romanians melted away at the first hint of conflict. It was like jousting with shadows. The worst enemy I never bested."

Years later when I left Romania his memory was burned with the branding iron of fear into the sailors of Constanta. When I would go down to the harbor to look after my vessel, awkwardly stilted on the hard, their mouths would whisper half in terror, half in awe, "Where is Captain Tristan?" but their eyes would be saying, "God grant that he never returns."

The second tale of Tristan has become legend among the sailors of the Mediterranean. Tristan was on his way east in hot and improbable pursuit of yet one more improbable goal. I met up with him in the harbor of Rhodes. We wined and dined and lied a little to each other. I showed him how to tune his ham radio and he taught me some stuff about writing. We had a good, comradely few days and when the time came for him to sail east (eventually toward Tibet: he swore it was possible to sail up the Yangtze to those distant mountains), I was sad. I would miss him. It would be a little lonely even in the sardine can that Rhodes calls a harbor.

Those of you who have been to that tiny harbor know it is a magnet for the thousands of boats on the Mediterranean. It services not only yachts, but workboats, fisherboats, and the big liner ferryboats which web the islands of Greece together. The yachts are ranged out from the quay three deep. The first is tied to the quay, the second to the first, and the third hangs off the stern of the second. It is a mess, crowded and noisy and subject to heroic, Gordian tangles of nylon rodes and anchor chains. But it is a lovely place and all the yachts want to be there.

On the September day that Tristan was to depart, *precisely at noon*, there was a special crowding as a fleet of cruising sailboats and a flock of ferries had all arrived together the day before. You could almost walk across the harbor from boat to boat with dry feet.

On this day, feeling sentimental about Tristan's leaving, I was compelled to mark the moment with a ceremony that would ease my sense of loss and send Tristan on his way with warmth and memories. So I spent the morning visiting the thirty British boats in the harbor and, with them, hatched a plot.

Tristan was to depart at noon through the narrow harbor opening over which, in classical days, Colossus had stood. The plan was that all of the British boats in defer-

ence to a great British sailor would, at a signal, let loose
horns and whistles in an auditory frenzy of farewell. The
die was cast, the plot was hatched and we all waited, fingers hovering over buttons, for OUTWARD LEG (for so was
Tristan's boat called in memory of a lost leg of his own) to
push out of harbor.

The sun crested and Tristan, watch in hand and precise as usual, weighed anchor and motored the few
crowded yards toward the entrance. As the first inch of his
hull lined up in the narrow entrance, I gave the signal and,
as one Englishman, thirty horns and whistles were raised
in sycophantic salute.

But I had underestimated the passion of the other hundreds of Mediterranean yachts in harbor and had forgotten
that Tristan's reputation stretched far beyond his own
Blessed Isles. The boats instantly caught on to what was
afoot and our thirty whistles were joined by two hundred
others in a cacophony of farewells, a screaming spate of
sound and sentiment. The big ferries vroomed, the fisherboats screeched, the workboats hooted and the yachts,
with their electronic whoopers, created such an ado, that
the noise alone seemed to push a flushed and surprised
Tristan through the harbor entrance.

That was the moment that the departed Colossus (or
perhaps Poseidon himself) chose to remind us that hubris
at sea was no less tricky than hubris on land. With a deft
flick of an astral hand, a trailing line was wound tightly
around Tristan's prop and OUTWARD LEG came to a full,
lurching stop in mid-exit among screams of adulatory
farewells and in a perfect deluge of unforgettable embarrassment.

It simply was not fair. With every eye in the Mediterranean turned upon him so basic an accident should not
have struck. Lines wound around props are for tyros on
fat charter boats, not for a veteran of circumnavigations
and countless adventures. But Tristan rose to the occasion,

bowed to his raucous court, and quietly turned to the cumbrous task at hand.

He sent his young crew member overboard with a knife to free OUTWARD LEG. The young man popped to the surface, trailing severed lines, and holding high over his head a mysterious, dripping, unidentifiable bundle. Tristan sailed out but not before he bellowed to those ashore, "Ha! The gods have a queer way to have us mortals do their work. I have found the lost head of the Colossus! I will write about it in my next book."

He never did but maybe he was saving the head for a final book of improbabilities that poor Tristan never got to write. Underestimate Tristan at your peril, gentlemen, at your peril.

As for me, I learned the sailorly lesson that what happens at sea has only the heavens as a forgiving audience but what happens in harbor chances the judgment of peers. I also learned how to snatch victory from the dripping jaws of defeat with elegance and aplomb.

MELEK AND THE WEDDING KILIM

To fully appreciate this tale of Turkish commercial acumen, you must first know just a little about me. I have been a salesman all of my life. I know how to sell people things. I know what buttons of acquisitive greed to push. I am a consummate peddler, a condition that my father used to describe as being "neither a great honor nor a small disgrace." From my vast experience of compelling customers to disgorge large sums for gewgaws that they could as easily have done without, I should damn well have known better.

When, after too many decades, I became fed up with peddling, I dumped it all, businesses, wives and children, bought a sailing vessel, and went sailing around the world. That is how I found myself in the harbor of Antalya.

As a merchant I had long since trained my eye to the glories of the Kilim, flat woven rugs of ancient designs that had come out of the mountains of Iraq, Iran and Turkey for half a millennium. Kilim come in a bewildering array of patterns and qualities since every village had its own production and every clan its own pattern. It was easy to recognize a good Kilim from a bad one. Recognizing the great from the good, as in all art matters, was another problem altogether.

I knew that Antalya had been a market place for great Kilim with generations of rug merchants hiding the very best from buyers till nothing else would do. This reluctance to sell became my undoing.

Melek, the rug merchant, had grown old and wily in his craft. He could smell money, detect instantly denials of wealth, and had the patience of ancient peasants when it came to bargaining. Melek had an exquisite sense of timing and like a great fisherman he knew when the fish had been played to exhaustion and the moment for reeling in had arrived.

I wanted an Iranian Kilim of some age. These are rare, and when they appear they are hoarded for a truly demanding buyer. I sat with Melek in one of his three shops and drank myself to the edge of diabetes with the syrupy sweet Turkish tea that never slakes your thirst. I was shown hundred of carpets, all which, although some were delicious, I waved away with the Turkish word for 'trash'. I thought that I was beginning to annoy Melek, but, as it turned out, it was more like a fisherman annoying a hooked fish, with me being the fish.

On the second day of my quest, I found Melek sitting disconsolately in his shop. He confessed that I had worn him down and that he had hidden away a great wedding Kilim from Iran, "so soft that the entire carpet can be folded into one hand." He was, he claimed, saving the wedding Kilim as a dowry for his own daughter but, since I was so knowledgeable, he agreed to let me see it. Not to buy it "at any price," but only for the joy of sharing such beauty with another devotee of the art.

I had never even dared to hope for a wedding Kilim, that was beyond even my greedy dreams and Melek knew it. The hint that there existed an ancient Iranian wedding Kilim in Antalya, more desirable because it was not for sale, set me ablaze.

The rat that I should have smelled earlier became a man-eater. I was well and truly hooked and the gaff was about to be set.

Melek took me to a hidden, private room in a far part of the city. It was small with no signs that it was a business. Inside there were no rugs, just a curtain at one end and hookas and tea tables scattered about.

We sat and smoked, drank more tea, and finally Melek arose and with the *hauteur* of a Michelangelo exposing the Ceiling, he swept aside the curtain to reveal, not a Kilim as I had expected, but a safe as big as the Ritz. I was impressed. I was wiped out by the drama.

The plot was one that I could have, and indeed, had written for my own 'pigeons' as I softened them up for the kill. The great safe was the final touch. I salivated all over a silken floor carpet as Melek, slowly, with seeming reluctance, turned the dials on the safe.

When the vault door creaked open it revealed an enormous cavern, totally empty save for one small silk wrapped bag. Melek reverentially opened the bag and with infinite tenderness he unfolded the most glorious Kilim I had ever seen or ever imagined.

It was, he reminded me, not for sale. It was insured, he claimed, at Lloyd's for $20,000. I offered $1,000 if he would sell and he looked at me with such disdain that I immediately doubled my offer. "Not for sale. For my precious Sabrina on her wedding day." I doubled again and again. The price was now enough to buy 'precious Sabrina' any house in Antalya. "Impossible," Melek croaked but even he could not hide the little dollars signs dancing in his eyes. I needed a clincher.

"I'll pay you in gold," I triumphantly declared, knowing that in the Near East, gold has blinding power. I watched poor Melek twist (so I thought) on my golden rope. "But my daughter," he cried, "my precious Sabrina. I cannot do this to her."

But in the end he did. I took my little carpet, tinkled out thousands of dollars in gold coins, and rushed to my boat.

The next day, away from Melek's magic skills, I sensed that I had been hustled. The carpet was superb, but I had paid twice the price that any carpet ever brought in Turkey no matter what its quality or age.

I thought out Melek but he had vanished with his entire entourage and all my gold. I had been had. Served me right. I'd had my comeuppance as a peddler.

Back in the U.S. the next year, I reluctantly unfolded the carpet for a real expert and waited for him to tell me how foolish I had been. His eyes widened and without a pause he offered me five times the enormous sum that I had paid.

I had learned before I sailed from Turkey that there was no 'daughter Sabrina', only sons, and that Melek was known as the slyest rug merchant in Turkey. I came away with two great gifts: a truly remarkable Kilim and the knowledge that I had the chastising pleasure of being taught a lesson by a great master.

It is not often in a hustle that both the hustler and the hustlee end up doing very well.

GHUDU AND THE RIVER GODS

On the banks of the Chappora river lies the other India, as different from Bombay and Calcutta as is Appalachia from New York City. It is the India of the villages in which *l'ancien régime* lingers and persists.

It had rained for the six months of the monsoon. The river mouth was silted up and the water was clogged with the thick, rich loam stripped from farmland to the east. The bottom of our 46-foot UNLIKELY, fed by the soil and by the untreated droppings of humankind and cattlekind up river, had grown a shaggy beard of living things. UNLIKELY was encrusted from stem to stern with life we could not even name. It was necessary to haul her out of the water and scrape and repaint her bottom.

We were trapped by the monsoon in an ancient river behind a dam of silt. We were anchored off a village already a thousand years old when the first Portuguese arrived. There was no marine railway, no steel cables, no scuba gear and no one who had even dreamed of hauling 25 tons of expensive, frangible fiberglass out of the river. But the job needed doing.

The entire village of Goudan began an exhaustive, if inapplicable, discussion of the problem. No aspect of the task was left uninvestigated although it was evident that the discussers had not the faintest notion of the real problems involved. As the talk grew the project escaped my control. It added excitement and variety to the life of the villagers. They now had large business to do, in place of the small routines of centuries. One way or another, it became clear that the village had adopted UNLIKELY. They had accepted the challenge to haul her. It now became a matter of honor.

Besides the novelty, the project brought into play conflicts between families and individuals which might have gone back a century or two. Which ideas were workable and, most important, who would get the dizzying honor of doing the job, sharpened claims and opinions. Too many egos and too much 'face' was at stake. My accidental and innocent presence was to alter the village of Goudan forever.

While the whole village proposed schemes, one more outlandish and less likely to succeed than the next, the choice revived an old struggle between two of the leading men of the village. Both were members of the same family. Modu was the richest man in the village and the other, Ghudu, the poorest.

Modu, the village capitalist, had been a poor man of good birth. He had struggled to accumulate the pittance needed to indulge in entrepeneurship. He had acquired a motorcycle, a television set, an electric fan, a 'great truck' (leased out to a gravel pit) and a 40-foot fishing trawler which, in season, was sent out to seine for shrimp, the universal protein of the poor. Modu owned these great riches by himself. "No father, no brother, Modu own alone." he liked to boast. The other seiners in the river were family efforts, but not Modu's. "Modu own alone."

His present wealth was only seven years old and had come about, as do most things, in grasping at a stroke of fortune. Modu's good luck had been Ghudu's bad luck. Ghudu had been, at that time seven years before, the wealthiest man in village. Ghudu had owned the fishing trawler now owned by Modu but, a passionate gambler, he had lost it on a roll of the dice. Modu, though poor, had been able to borrow, at very high interest, enough money from relatives to take the trawler at a great bargain. Although life in the villages changes almost not at all, when it does change there are no mechanisms of moderation, no ways to resist reversal. So as Modu's fortunes suddenly leapt up, just so quickly had Ghudu's descended.

The great 'ship hauling problem' provided another

confrontation between these two, so obviously tied together by the stars. Both had owned the same fishing trawler, so both were now great marine experts. The village was divided on which of these two important persons would do the deed. I was not consulted.

Modu also owned the only truck in the village and it was his loudly stated opinion that a slipway of logs should be built on the river bank and he, with the aid of his 'great truck', would haul UNLIKELY up the slipway while the men of the village kept her propped upright with logs. I had seen the 'great truck' and my heart was heavy for my beloved boat. I had also seen groups of co-operating Indian workmen pulling in every direction but the right one.

Ghudu was more devious. He knew his villagers well and he knew that ultimately it would be they, not I, who would make the final choice. He knew their love of a puzzle, a mystery. He knew of their bottomless need for entertainment. He would win the day with magic.

Ghudu refused to reveal what he called his 'great plan'. Only if he were chosen to do the job would his neighbors learn the secret. He threw out irresistible bait.

"I will bring the boat out of the water and put it back in only twelve hours," he boasted, "and I will do it alone." To a stunned audience he added: "With only the help of the old gods of the river I will do this. No trucks, no machines. Only four stout logs and a bit of hemp will be needed to assist the river gods." With that he shut his mouth, folded his arms, and refused to respond to derision from one side and curiosity from the other. He had his audience eating out of his hand.

But Modu, puzzled by the boast, felt he was being outmaneuvered. Nevertheless, he seized upon the moment as a means of profit. If he, Modu, could not do the job, then Ghudu would somehow have to be made to pay.

"If the man who speaks so intimately with the old gods is so sure that he can raise this vessel out of the water, by himself, as he boasts, and put it back, again by himself, in twelve hours, will he accept a wager?"

The village knew Ghudu's history and his passion for gambling. They watched his eyes gleam with the old fever too long denied to him as a poor man on the edge of starvation. He was back in business. "Stakes?" he asked.

"If you do as you boast, and let the village be the judge, I will wager your fishing boat which I now own."

"And should you win, what is it that I will have to give you?"

"Your labor for seven years."

A serious wager. An uneven wager. Should Ghudu lose his family might well starve. Should Modu lose he would only lose his boat. He would still have his 'great truck'. His family would not be threatened.

The village, gathered to view this final clash, recognized cunning Modu's challenge to the life of a family and the freedom of a man. Things had swept not only out of my control, but out of control of the village itself. As the murmurs of protest against the unfairness of Modu's intent began to sweep through the villagers, Ghudu rose and silenced them.

"On my word, on my heart, and on the lives of my children, I accept the wager. But with one condition."

The Modu faction nodded wisely to each other. Ghudu had lost. He would now destroy his honor with an impossible condition and everyone would know. Better for Ghudu that he lose his freedom and his family in failure than lose his good name forever.

"The task," said Ghudu quietly, "must be done on the day following the full moon. That is my condition."

"Accepted," Modu instantly replied.

The wager was on. A titanic battle had been joined between the two most important men in Goudan. My own part of the wager was the very existence of my boat. But that no longer counted, even to me. The stakes were now too high. No one could match Ghudu's risk. I, along with the rest of the villagers, became audience.

It was three weeks to the full moon. All eyes were on Ghudu, expecting furious preparations. Ghudu went into the forest and cut four stout logs, each fifteen feet long, dragged them back and left them on the river bank just above the tide line. Then he rested. Nothing more. For three weeks he dawdled with his children and worked his little bit of land. He did not even seem to pray any harder than was his habit. It was as if Ghudu had forgotten the wager. Modu counted his winnings.

On the night of the full moon, always a special time in India, a great feast was given by Modu to which the whole village was invited. The feast lasted throughout the moonbright night and, as the sun rose, Ghudu, followed by the entire village, sauntered down to the shore.

Ghudu waded out up to his neck in the high tide and sank his first log in the mud parallel to the shore line. He pulled the bow of UNLIKELY as close to shore as possible, setting the keel upon the middle of the log on the river bottom. He then laid another log on deck parallel to the log in the mud and tied the portside ends together and the starboard ends together with heavy strands of his hemp rope. He tightened them by twisting and wetting the lines. The rope shrunk and the parallel logs were pulled firm on deck and keel. He repeated the same at the aft end of UNLIKELY and when he was finished he had my boat sandwiched between two sets of logs making a solid frame in which she could safely be held upright. Safe, that is, if Ghudu was able to raise UNLIKELY out of the water and set her on ground.

In two hours, his labor with the logs finished, Ghudu stretched out on the river bank and treated himself to the expensive luxury of a cigarette, a real cigarette that he had not rolled himself. He rested and smoked and waited as the villagers grew impatient. When they complained, he quieted them with the reminder that he had twelve hours.

An hour passed and then another and then, as if at the hands of the river gods, exactly as Ghudu had promised, UNLIKELY majestically rose, unaided, out of the river.

Ghudu won his wager, won back his boat, was again a rich man and, at least for the moment and sweetest of all, he had bested his old foe.

Note: The method was simple. The full moon tide—which was the condition of the bet—lowered the river just enough to deposit UNLIKELY on the brace of logs that had been tied, parallel, fore and aft. The river gods, at the behest of Ghudu, had done their job.

CHAPTER EIGHT

Keeled Beloveds

LIKE OUR SOFTER MATES on shore, our boats comfort and protect the sailor from the wild chaos without. And like our mates they are our keeled beloveds.

I have had three keeled beloveds. All three boats had a hand in teaching me to sail and, in dire straits, saving me from myself. I owe them my high sense of pleasure in life. I owe them most of the latter decades of my existence which, I absolutely believe, would not have been mine had I not been a sailor.

GODSMILE taught me humility in the face of the sea, UNLIKELY VII carried me triumphantly around the world, and HEARTFELT, near the end of my own passage through life, finally taught me that the essence of life was not the big stuff of which our pasts might be structured, but the small and immediate pleasures of going back once more into the sea.

These vessels span my life at sea, the 40 years spent mostly in confusion but always in awe of my good fortune of being a sailor.

GODSMILE

She was a little sloop with no name. I had bought her on a whim, all 22 feet of her. She was vintage fiberglass, well found as most early glass boats were, but rusty and gored in places and rotten down below. Her beauty had been obscured by dirt and disuse.

I bought her by accident, the way good things happen. I was answering an advertisement for a modern 24 footer but I became confused over the address. I pulled into the wrong front yard and there was the wrong boat, waiting for me. The right underbody, the right age, the right rig, the right size, and, upon a little inspection, truth in building.

Her owner was as confused as I was. He had not advertised her for sale and I kept insisting that he had. He would like to be rid of her but she was "too much trouble to sell." He viewed the boat as a total liability and me as a total loony, but when I was able to convince him that, although confused, I was serious, he said "How about $3000?" I heard the question mark and I knew I had my boat. In the best haggling tradition I offered $1500 and quickly settled for $1800 because eighteen, being the Hebrew symbol for life, is a mystical number.

I hauled my nameless waif to my own backyard and, contrary to all advice I have ever given or received, I did my survey after I bought her. I had got what I had got and I was resolved to love her. She had a cast iron keel (rare these days) and lovingly laid fiberglass put in with a heavy hand. She had yards of varnished mahogany below, an outboard rudder of heroic dimensions and 27 feet of elegantly extruded aluminum mast. She had been built in France a decade and a half earlier. The name of her class was Golif.

Her companionway hatch and frame were rotted away and she had great holes torn in her fiberglass deck where she had stove herself, unattended, in some forgotten storm. She had a leaky, rusty iron water tank and electrics that Tom Edison would have rejected. She was a disaster. She was exactly right.

Since this is the tale of how my boat was named I will resist a recital of reconstruction. But total reconstruction it was. I was infected with the virus of renovation. From keel to masthead, from pulpit to pushpit, every thing I could think of doing, or redoing, was done, including, for reasons obscure even to myself at the moment, replacing an old but usable 6-hp outboard with a new and unecessarily powerful 9-hp model equipped with a large, slow turning, three-bladed prop. And well I had. But more of this later.

I rebuilt her on Long Island. Her maiden passage was planned as a leisurely, easy sail down the East River and along the familiar coast of New Jersey to Atlantic City, my hailing port. My son Gil, a good sailor (high praise from a salty father) and a friend of his, Jesse, were to crew with me. A newly rebuilt boat, a strong young crew, and a picnic jaunt down a short stretch of coast to which I was no stranger. Piece of cake.

Before departing Long Island I did some things right and a number of things very wrong. In the right column was the fortuitous purchase of the new outboard. In the wrong column was retaining the roller-furling gear that came with the boat. I had long relegated roller furling to that long list of no-nos to which old sailors cling, mostly out of suspicion of newness. Anything so convenient as pulling a line to furl a sail had to have in it the seeds of disaster.

I have also held battens in disrespect. I was soon to be educated in an entirely unanticipated danger from the use of battens.

Most reprehensible was my failure to attend to weather forecasts. I had checked a three-day forecast and it had seemed fine. I had lazily ignored the fact that the closer to land the more dangerous short term weather can be. I should have checked local weather every three hours, not three days.

We sailed off into the Sound on Sunday morning for the two-day downhill run to home. It was a hot and humid day dominated by a wind from the south, always a harbinger of unsettled weather. We caught the tide and were squirted down the East River and whipped through Hell's Gate, hairy for a 22 footer, but a ride I strongly recommend.

We were flung out into the Upper Bay in the late afternoon. The wind had eased and the chances of rounding Sandy Hook before dark faded with the fading breeze. Just as we slipped under the Verrazzano Bridge the sun set and a bank of fog dropped on us like a curtain. I later learned that the fog had been predicted and small craft warnings were broadcast.

Bar the Red Sea, this was the worst place to be. It was night and we were in a dense fog in the middle of the Ambrose Light big boat channel. Nothing is more frightening to a small boat sailor than the bow of a black freighter looming uncaringly out of a fog. Except perhaps hearing big boats close at hand and not being able to see them at all. Several barely missed us as we heard them slip past in the fog. They could not see us and, as for hearing us, our 'peep peep' was no contest to their 'vroom vroom'.

I headed at what I hoped was 90 degrees across the channel. As we had not had time to rig the depthfinder, and as visibility still extended only to the mast, I asked my son to throw the lead. Depth, I thought, was the only hint I would have of proximity to Staten Island. At that moment, eerily, a bonfire loomed out of the murk. Some youngsters were having a beach party and their bonfire was a welcome, if illegal, beacon. We were barely a boat's length off shore, in just a foot over our draw. I dropped the hook and breathed for the first time since we hit the fog.

The anchorage was uncomfortable. There was a bad chop and heavy swells from passing freighters. The anchor held but I had had no chance to test its grip as the shore had come up too quickly. It was time to rapidly down all sail. The roller jib furled neatly but as we let the main halyard go the main refused to come down. It stayed stubbornly and firmly up the mast, held by a jammed shackle. The main had been cut a whisker too long, allowing the halyard shackle to jam into the sheave at masthead.

"No problem," said I, "let go the outhaul, pull the foot off the boom and furl the main around the mast." However there was a problem, more precisely, four of them. The battens, out of our reach from the cockpit, were acting as little booms, holding the sail into the wind and making it unfurlable. My son had to go up the mast to free the shackle. He managed, but just barely. Beware of battens. Without them we could have easily furled the main to the mast. With them we could just as easily have joined the party on the beach.

The next morning, still ignorant of the terrors ahead, we rounded Sandy Hook and sailed into a gentle breeze on our nose. This wind from an unexpected direction required our outboard and reduced our fuel supply. Somewhere down the coast we would need more fuel. The charts showed Shark River Inlet just within range of our remaining fuel.

All was going well when suddenly the sky ahead turned a ragged, angry black that speaks of unpleasant winds. The darkening clouds were low and staccato with lightning. It was so unexpected, so fast and so complete a change that it was as if we had been sailing two separate passages, one unrelated to the other.

I have been through my share of squalls and have taken my measure of them and they of me. I don't underestimate them. Woe to the sailor who does. But this one harbored a nastiness I had never seen, my crew had little experience with lightning, and to make matters worse, shore—which could easily become lee—was only a mile off.

Lightning, I reassured my crew, rarely strikes small boats. They were unimpressed and hastened to remove all sail. The main came down smartly this time and the jib properly wound itself around its roller wire. However, as the wind had come up a sudden howler, the roller jib tightened around the headstay and we ran out of control line before the entire jib was furled. A small triangle remained, usually no problem except that in minutes the winds screamed up to 60 knots in that first squall and the 'little triangle' became a serious threat to the safety of the boat. This first squall was the most vicious of all my years of sailing and the next three were worse.

As the wind struck us I watched, with horror, the little triangle quickly enlarge itself as the increasing force of the wind continued to 'windowshade' the jib around the forestay. Suddenly there was more sail aloft than the little boat could handle. We were overpowered and the wind continued to rise. We were unable to hold a course, and that little triangle of canvas, even with loosed sheets, laid our boat out on its beam ends. We were in trouble.

It was impossible to get onto the foredeck to bring the jib down. All I could do was pray that the rebuilding had been sound.

The first squall lasted half an hour. We had no time to worry about the lightning that danced about us since the task of staying aboard our out-of-control boat used up all our energies. We were at the mercy of the wind and that damned roller *un*furling jib. The jib finally tore along a seam, easing the pressure a bit, and, at the same moment, the wind halted, literally to a screeching stop, as quickly as it had appeared.

The lightning had not let up and as we looked to the south there was an even blacker squall about to roll over us. In the short lull we got the demon triangle down and trimmed the boat a bit just as the wind leaped again to fury. To further test our love of sailing, the second storm dumped endless sheets of blinding rain on us. The rain was so dense that visibility hardly extended beyond an outstretched arm.

Acutely aware of shore less than a mile to the west, I was able to put the bow to the southeast and held her there with the blessed new outboard for the half hour of the second storm. But the following two storms were of such fury that our course and our heading became totally out of our control.

As visibility returned after the second storm we saw the third bearing down upon us. It began to seem as if they would never let up and my fears for the untested boat grew with each blow. I had never been more frightened in all my time at sea. The third storm seemed interminable. It lasted for an hour and it was all we could do to keep the seas out of the boat. Time and again we lost our sense of direction and found ourselves headed toward the looming shore. The winds exceeded 60 knots (later confirmed by the weather bureau) and came at us from all directions at once. I started to consider the possible need to beach the boat. The winds built and the rain blinded us. The lightning was incessant and the strikes so close to the boat that we were repeatedly bathed by blasts of hot air. At times we breathed the pure ozone manufactured by lightning, an eerie but curiously exhilarating experience.

As the third storm waned and visibility returned, we found ourselves, miraculously and accidentally, within ten yards of the buoy for Shark River Inlet just half a mile to the west. I gratefully turned the little boat toward the safe harbor, now so visible and so near, when the ultimate storm, numerically and in intensity, broke upon us. It was too much. We were so close. This was the fourth squall of the procession in whose path we lay. Its winds were 80 knots, later confirmed, and it spun us so violently that the compass, when we could see it through the sheets of rain, had no chance to even damp itself. The boat assumed its beam ends, without the assist of a 'little triangle'.

This tale is not about the rebuilding of a sailboat nor is it about the survival of that vessel in terrible weather. It is about how my little boat got its name. It happened during the fourth of the four squalls and had there not been three of us aboard, and if all three had not agreed down to the smallest detail of what we saw, I would not ask the reader to strain credulity. We saw what we saw, and for whatever it is worth, I share it with you.

The fourth storm had closed down on us when we were within tasting distance of the entrance to Shark River. We immediately lost our bearings again and, as it sometimes happens in storms such as this, the wind dropped and the sky momentarily opened in the east. There, in the sky, painted in sure and solid black strokes of cloud against the lighter clouds beyond, appeared a face. The face was about 30 degrees above the horizon and about 10 degrees in diameter. All three of us saw a large round visage with round dark eyes surely and evenly drawn under a broad, clear forehead. Below a small nose was a long downward sweeping moustache which blended into a huge white beard. It was the classic image associated with the old testament God of the Hebrews.

And a god who, at this moment, was wearing a fierce and accusing frown.

None of the three of us are particularly religious. But as the wind returned and tore at the face, it changed from its original frown of fierce disapproval, just before it disappeared back into the black storm, to a wide, warm and reassuring smile. At that moment, we all knew that everything was going to be okay.

Irrational? Sure. A bit of communal delirium? Perhaps. An accident of cloud and wind? Call it what you will, but we saw what we saw.

Later, safe and warm at dinner, a little drunk, with wives and friends around us to hear the tale of our small adventure, I reminded the table that our craft had no name. There was silence for a long, long moment as we all became aware that the brave little boat deserved a worthy name.

The silence stretched out, and then someone whispered GODSMILE.

And our little waif had her name.

HEARTFELT

Some time ago, through age and circumstance, I was cast upon the shore.

I was forced to bring my beloved cutter, UNLIKELY, to what I fervently hope will be a temporary stay in Key West. This sad event was precipitated by a torn shoulder complicated by 75 years of normal attrition. I must confess that the shoulder was only part of the problem as I had managed a small heart attack two years ago. The heart attack might not have stopped me. The shoulder has and will for a little time to come.

Bereft, even for a few months, of my life asea I sensed a looming mortality. I was advised by landlubbed and unfeeling medics not to sail my 46 footer till my shoulder healed. They had, I mourned, consigned me to a geriatric trash pile. Thrash about as I might, the trash pile of age loomed ever closer. I told them that I would rather be buried at sea and they informed me they would rather I not be buried at all since my time had not yet come. I replied that being ashore made my time feel like a lot shorter than at sea.

I refuse to accept my implied demise. I am, however,

unable to either grow younger or to permanently repair
heart and shoulder, and thus get back to a condition into
which I could again cross oceans in a sailboat.

Unable to reverse time and disability I mused on a
more arrogant solution. Perhaps the answer was to become a born again sailor. If folk, I reasoned, could, by a
simple declaration, be born again as an immaculately new
person in the eyes of the Lord, could I not be born again
as a new sailor? Certainly it should be easier to merely rebirth a new sailor than to rebirth a whole tangled new
person.

Problem is that you need no vehicle to become a new
person but a sailor needs a boat and I had been forbidden,
for the time being, my 46 footer. But the medics did not go
into specifics as to what, if anything, I *could* sail and, as
we all know, the devil is in the details.

I cast myself back in time to my first serious little
boat, a Greenwich 24, which taught me how to sail. I went
out and bought a Coronado 25 of the same vintage, reasoning that the gods were not so unfeeling as to deny me
one more measly foot.

After sailing a 22-ton, 46-foot cutter in what I now
considered was my 'previous' life, tootling about in 25 feet
was child's play, which is what I declared my self to be . . .
a reborn child playing about in the sea.

Then came the need for naming the little vessel which
had arrived fully equipped but *sans* name. I have always
believed that it is okay to name a powerboat any old damn
fool name, such as the one a neighbor, a dedicated fisherman, inelegantly named GRUNT MOLESTER. But when it
comes to sailboats, names must be serious, elegant and respectful.

The little 25 footer came into my life as a result of a
heart attack so, with a doff of the hat to the sea gods, she
has become HEARTFELT, a tender and wistful reminder that
things could be worse. The little boat could just as well
have been called SHOULDER TO THE WHEEL or even A SHOUL-

DER TO LEAN ON but these names were somehow not sufficiently poetic. HEARTFELT is both poetic and evocative of
the event that brought her to me so HEARTFELT she is and
will forever be.

What a delight she is. I toyed with the conceit of no
motor at all. My solution was the smallest, lightest, and
simplest of all marine propulsion devices, a battery oper-
ated trolling motor. With it I can get back up channel
when the wind is converse. The bonuses of an electric
motor are no noise, no stink, no pollution, and, of course,
no speed which I view to be the major advantage of a
small motor.

Besides, there should not be anywhere that I cannot
go in 25 feet of nimble sailboat. Even tacking up a 35-foot
wide channel is doable with patience and concentration.

Therefore, to all you sailorly ancients who are bound
up with medical restraints, just remember that, while your
doctors view you as old and creaky, in your heart of
hearts you are simply "a young man with something
wrong with you."

So give the young man still inside you the gift again of
a first small sailboat, and let it teach once more the simple,
life enhancing joys of sailing.

UNLIKELY FINDS A HOME

We were returning after 17 years of a circumnavigation.
We had spent the last two years in Cuba and when Castro
showed so little good sense as to shoot down American
planes, we left for the States.

It was, anyway, time to come home. Our vessel, UN-
LIKELY, a 46 footer from the pen of Ted Brewer, had not
been home since we fitted her out in Miami in 1979. She
and I were aging, she most gracefully, and I perhaps not
so. I began to feel the need for a small piece of American

earth. A place in the States to settle in for a bit after the alarums and excursions on the wilder shores of passage making.

The problem was where. The States proved astonishingly expensive after the Third World. I wanted UNLIKELY by our side wherever we settled and that meant we had to find evermore scarce shoreline. Marina life suited neither of us. It was too social and too expensive, so we started out to find a solution that was both within our budget and gave us access to UNLIKELY.

I came up with a brilliant idea. We were to find a piece of property in the Keys which we could buy, tie up UNLIKELY and live aboard her. Problem was that there are few places in all the Keys that will accommodate a six-foot draft.

We had almost given up when we found a sensational lot on Key West right on the Atlantic just a few miles east of the city. It was completely out of the tourist zone and bordered by a deep canal. Best of all, the canal emptied directly into the Atlantic and the entry would, with a bit of weather eye to the moon, take our six-foot draft.

Alas, the property was not for sale, our real estate agent sadly informed us. Indeed it had not been for sale for 20 years and was unlikely to ever become available. We departed dejectedly.

At 10 A.M. the next morning the agent phoned.

"I understand that your vessel is called UNLIKELY."

"Yes," we replied, puzzled why he had asked.

"As I told you the site you asked about was most unlikely to come up for sale."

"So?" we queried.

"Well, like your boat's name, the unlikeliest thing in my experience happened this morning. After 20 years of being off the market the lot you want came into my office for sale. Do you want it?"

"Buy it! " we screeched and that evening we had bought our dream place. All of our problems of where to dock UNLIKELY and where to live in the Keys were solved. Hallelujah!

But, as the saying goes, "Man plans and God laughs." He was surely chortling away that day since, after buying the property, we were informed by the Monroe County code enforcement inspector that no one could live aboard on the canal and, what was worse, no boat could be permanently docked on a property that had no house.

We were the owners of a piece of expensive land on which we could not live aboard UNLIKELY and hundreds of feet of concrete bulkhead where we could not even dock UNLIKELY.

What to do? The obvious, of course! Build a little house.

But because of the stringency attached to the granting of permits in the Keys our 'little house' acquired the equivalence of battlements and spires at the same speed that our bank accounts ebbed.

Luckily the ebbing stopped at ground zero just as the last code-required improvement was put in place. We now have a hurricane proof, reinforced concrete abode which is bordered 20 feet to port by a deep canal and 20 feet to starboard by the blue Atlantic. Our nearest neighbor to the east is 3000 miles away.

The house took a year to build but the day finally came when we were able to bring UNLIKELY alongside and secure her to concrete in a protected canal. At breakfast, on the front porch perched 15 feet above the flood plain, we are able to look down on our beloved vessel and recall the great passages of the past and plan the ones to come.

CHAPTER NINE

Sailorly Stuff

IN TRUTH THE FOLLOWING essays belong in a different book. They are included because they please me more than most of my scribbles and because I quietly wriggled them in when my editor was occupied elsewhere. And while these pieces do not deal with individuals, they talk of groups, some sort of averages of the different faces of sailordom.

A writer, ultimately, writes to please himself, not necessarily his audience, and certainly not to please his editor. Therefore I take as my right to include stuff in this book that a publisher might have expunged.

Any sailor writing on the sea, to be worth his salt, must view his watery world through a lens wider than personal observations. He must be able to draw some sort of lesson, strike some chords of experience that twang in both sailors and non-sailors. This is done best in perceptive novels but I, unable to do fiction, which is very hard indeed, choose these bantam vignettes to make what I hope will be generic commentary.

A NEW BREED

Not until World War II came to its panting halt was it possible for any but the most remarkable of folk to approach sailing as a source of gratification. The racing of boats, which supplies its own bizarre gratifications rarely having to do with taking pleasure of the sea, has been around a bit longer. The origin of ocean racing lies in commercial competition; who could get to the fish 'fustest with the mostest' and never mind the misery for the crew. The tea clippers, in their epic, competing passages to and from the Indies, and their sister ships which rounded the Horn, or land marched across the Isthmus, all had to do with the incestuous equation that time and money are related. The faster, the more profit to owners. The faster, the more agony and danger to crew.

With the advent of fiberglass, reasonably reliable electronics, Dacron sails and sheets, nylon rode and stainless steel, the sailing world changed and people could, for the first time in history, make the argument that sailing can be fun. Those of us who go to sea in small boats know better. Venturing into wind and wave is scary, cold, wet, nauseating, and even a little dangerous now and then. But we all do it, and keep doing it, so sailors must have found some pleasure that lay beyond all that pain.

The human psyche is such that what is reasonably possible becomes compulsively doable and what is doable with risk and pain becomes to many a paradoxical source of pleasure. It was the search for pleasure that drove hundreds of thousands to sell the ranch, learn port from starboard, and venture out to the sea. These folk knew that they just had to get into a boat. Fantasy, image, and reality came together like an orgasm the first time that their sailboat took a bone in her teeth and her tiller came alive with a mind of its own.

I think all this is a pretty good thing. It pleases me when large numbers of folk involve themselves in an activity in which, if there is any risk, it is only to themselves and not to the fragile ecosphere we live in. It is also rare that any gratification is as unlikely to impose on the rights and freedoms of our neighbors as is sailing. Sailing is a private matter between you and the sea or, if you are so inclined, between you and your god. It is an activity which costs the earth nanonic resources compared to the billion return of delights. Sailors use up nothing, they pass the natural world along to the next generation as they found it—a pretty thought that I would not mind carved in the stone above me.

Being full of years I am selfishly fond of the fact that sailing has almost no upper age limit. Nothing has to be done quickly on a sailboat and rarely is great strength needed. Should immoderate muscle be required, it is usually in circumstances where the sea would overcome the strongest of us. And how nice to have a physical activity in which you are a hero in the eyes of your grandchildren.

We are taking pleasure in an activity which becomes, as the decades progress, less and less dangerous. "Full fathom five my father lies" is heard now only from salty and bearded guitarists and rarely from bereaved children. Sailing is no longer a sentence. It is, instead, a welcome reprieve from the confines and importunate clamors of land.

This new species of sailors-for-pleasure, so recently aborning, already are dividing in two breeds. Which side of the line you fall upon depends on the subtle question of how you take your pleasure. That you take it has already been settled by the simple fact that you are reading this.

If you take your delights in achieving goals, getting to places at which you directed your vessel, and getting there in quick time and high *éclat*, then you are the direct descendant of all those iron men who sailed the seas for profit and glory. The game is the getting there. The new delights of a new land are your attraction and getting there smartly on your own bottom is your reward.

But if you hunger not after the port just ahead, and

miss not the port just abandoned, then you represent an entirely new breed who revels not in the getting to, but in the pure doing. You are a passage maker, a sailor to whom the glory is in being out there, in unhampered commune with nature and self. You are a process sailor to whom the act of passing across a hundred miles of water is sufficient for the day. You never go 'to' anywhere; rather you always go 'toward' somewhere. You never have a time you must be at a place; your place to be is the open sea itself.

You will likely make long passages, never having planned to sail further than Bimini and you will, as I did, sail around the world, quite by accident.

I applaud those driven folk who must make this port or that in this time or that, since I applaud all sailors.

But I choose the wanderers, the aimless ones, the Moitessiers, as my friends.

THE SECRET JOYS OF SAILING

"A sailor's joys are as simple as a child's."

Thus spoke Moitessier in *The Long Way*, a book that conveys more of the joys of sailing than of the dull business of how-to-do sailing.

His ebullient recantations of small thrills and large personal revelations are familiar to any who has sailed the deep oceans. His pleasure in a bird, a fish, a wisp of air after a calm, are really what ocean sailing is about. How dull is the business of "where I went" and "how I did it." What the ocean sailor cares about is how he feels at sea.

The transfer of technical sailorly information takes place between the sailor and his living vessel. It is from his ship that the lubber becomes a sailor after ten days and a thousand miles out at sea. It is a learning process which simply cannot be conveyed in print. What you read about sail handling is different from the joy of learning that takes place as your muscles sense the tension and the liveliness of the pull of your sheets.

Even less can be read about that instinctive tugging and tucking that takes place as you reef in a rising breeze. True, an old sailor can pass tricks and techniques, but that stuff only goes into your head. What is necessary is sailing lore that goes directly into your muscles.

One of the truly great joys of sailing, as Moitessier knew in his bones, is the melding and merging that joins skipper to tiller to vessel. Each dip and wallow, each pull and release impart volumes of information to muscles and heart. The stuff you learn in your muscles is never unremembered.

The ocean sailor recaptures those joys of childhood when every taste was new and every vision unique, when learning of the world came as a blinding rush that melts into endless revelation. The simple joys of childhood emerged from the newness of each experience. It is the lovely gift of sailing that reinvents newness for the sailor. Experiences that on land have become dulled with familiarity are renewed in the so aptly named cradle of the sea. We sailors are offered the inestimable gift of rebirth. We are Botticelli's Venus emerging from the sea, newly made, fresh and, in our minds, beautiful and filled with the beauty about us.

Like children, the sailor loses sense of time. We sailors on a long ocean passage have no limiting sense of future, only the endless rolling of the seas beneath us that promises to go on forever. We are granted a limited immortality, a doubling of the experiences of non sailorly folk.

One of the simple joys of sailing is the naming of our vessels. We do not name our houses or cars, nor do we have anything to do with naming the cities and the streets where we live. Even the naming of our children sometimes dismays as when a 'Grace' is fat and dumpy and an 'Angel' becomes anything but.

The names we give our boats are never a disappointment. We name our boats as children name the unseen, imagined playmates of their secret and unseen lives. My own vessel, UNLIKELY, was named when I sensed how strange it was that I, overweight, overmortgaged, and overburdened with cares of family, was about to set out across 3,000 miles of open ocean.

After 17 years of circumnavigation I found myself battling a minor heart attack. When that battle was won I came across an ancient little 25 footer to tootle about in. She was named, of course, HEARTFELT.

Our boats' names are our secret dreams of childhood. A Russian friend who grew up on the cold steppes of Siberia named his boat ARIZONA: he could imagine no place warmer and no place more unlike Siberia. Or the unselfconsciously named LA FORZA DEL DESTINO, a name only a kid could dream up. Or the surgeon who could not avoid the truth and honestly named his boat ELECTIVE SURGERY.

It is not the large events in our lives from which we derive the most coin of pleasure. The big stuff that happens depends too much on chance for us to honestly claim credit. It is the small events for which we can claim kudos that evoke the largest emotional response. Like a child who will find endless joy in a pile of sand on a beach the sailor must find his reward in the pure pleasure of small-ish events. Like a child whose emotions swing from tearful scary awe to pure and unrestrained euphoric laughter, the sailor too can allow release of all of his hidden, inner self, exposed only to a beloved shipmate or two, and insulated from the judgmental crescendos of the too crowded land.

At sea a sailor's freedom is a child's freedom, unrestricted, untrammeled and involved only in the event of sailing itself. The universe in a child's eyes, of which he is the master, is the far reaches of his sandbox. The sailor's universe, in which he is master and ruler, is not much further to the three-mile reach of his horizon.

A bit small, perhaps, but quite enough to return the largest joys as Moitessier, himself, well knew.

THE CHRISTMAS OCEAN

One boisterous evening in the Bahamas we sought shelter from a choppy sea behind an unnamed, too small to be charted, isle. We cautiously felt our way to 50 feet off the beach in the wind shadow of the island, and dropped our hook into a comfortable eight (our draft being six) feet of water. A little later the clouds scudded away, the wind dropped, and a glorious full moon rose out of the island's palms.

At dawn one early riser called the crew on deck to see what lay around us. It was an unnerving sight of a forest of coral heads, all about a foot above water and completely surrounding the boat. We lay in a small pool, six feet deep and less than two boat lengths in diameter. The full moon of the previous evening had raised the level of our piece of sea just enough to allow us to sail innocently up a narrow channel in the tide-hidden reef to where we dropped anchor in the only place that did not dry out on the low tide.

Marcus, my mate, whipped on his scuba and plumbed our problem. He reported that our route into the pool was about eight feet wide and now at low tide was only four feet deep. We were trapped till the next high tide.

Luck had shielded us from disaster. Being caught in a tidal pool off a lovely island for a couple of hours was no big deal, but had we strayed a few feet one way or the other as we came up to the reef-guarded island our lovely vessel might well be there still, holed, and held by the jealous coral.

If you were to chart the oceans of the world and color in red all those parts less than a fathom deep and in green all those more than a fathom, you would produce a chart which is already engraved into the mind of every sailor. The red says "You can't sail here." The green says "Sail in safety." Between the two would lie a Christmassy mix of red and green which screams DANGER!

It is fiction that sailboats are regularly lost in the vast spaces of the Pacific or, indeed, in the Bermuda Triangle of the Atlantic. Nor have any friends of mine ever sailed into trouble in the Indian Ocean or the South China Sea. But more than I want to count have lost their boats in the Christmas Ocean, that narrow band of water in which the red of too little water and the green of just enough mix and match. The Christmas Ocean begins where the first peak of sea bed rises to within six feet of the surface (while all about is comfortably deep) and ends when the green runs out and all the depths from there to land are less than a fathom.

In the deep oceans you point your bow and the wind carries you through an undistorted surface of a thousand fathoms of water. In the Christmas Ocean, as the sea bed starts sloping upward toward the jutting reefs, there is simply not sufficient water under your keel to smooth out the grip of the sea floor on the sea surface. It is here that seas get *steep,* a sailorly term for tumult and danger. A sea can be safely as tall as the Ritz so long as there is enough distance between crests to prevent their breaking. It is the breaking of the crest of a sea which can cause a thousand tons of water to bury you, or can cause your boat to lose its grip on the water and fall off the side of a wave.

This happens when the great and comfortable deep ocean rollers start to 'feel' a shallowing sea, when they get pushed closer together by the friction on their bottoms and their slopes become steeper until gravity deforms the shape of the wave and it collapses. You do not have to hit a reef; a breaking sea alone can do you in. And all breaking seas except those in 'ultimate storms' are denizens of the Christmas Ocean.

Also in the Christmas Ocean, because it is small and close to land and to the ports upon which all shipping converges, the traffic problem becomes acute. True, you could be run down by a freighter a thousand miles offshore but that would be an unlikely event helped along by either the most extreme stupidity on your part or some sensationally bad luck. More likely you will keep your appointment in Samarra thirty miles from land and a half day out of port.

If you do not get run down by something a hundred times larger than you, there is still the other possibility that you will destroy a small, badly-lighted fishing boat that somehow appeared under your bows. In some countries this is a very expensive way to enter port. The fisherman sunk by you usually retires and buys a third world version of a condominium in Florida on the largess dragged out of you by the courts of his country.

If neither of these catastrophes occur there remains the aggravating, and potentially dangerous, business of spiraling an unbreakable length of nylon from a lobster pot around your propeller. I did just that coming up on Bermuda on a dark night with traffic pounding all about me. I did it once more at the sand-strewn entrance to Cape Fear, also on a dark night (I guess there is no other kind), and also in a constricted and busy channel.

The dangers of the Christmas Ocean are legion, unexpected, and give little time for considered response. The difference between the Christmas Ocean and the deep oceans is having a hundred feet or a hundred miles in which to concoct a defense.

I have been in some of the more infamous Christmas Oceans of the world. The Yucátan Channel, through which the Gulf of Mexico and the northern Caribbean ebb and flow, is among the worst. Although deeper than a fathom it is relatively shallow and busy with traffic. Its fifty-mile width disallows navigational error. It is tight with pleasure boats seeking the big fish of Cozumel and merchant ships seeking the busy ports of Galveston and

New Orleans. Its narrowness increases the flow and ve-
locity of the current and its lack of depth creates seas
through which you can see the sun at noon.

The Straits of Mollucca, which separate Indonesia
from Singapore and Thailand, is one of the busiest of the
narrow, shallow places. The traffic is so heavy that you
could almost cross the Straits on a bridge of ships. These
shallow and busy waters are further complicated by the inhospitable countries which line either bank. Once you depart north from Singapore, head right for Sri Lanka.

No small boat has ever been pirated a hundred miles
offshore. Modern piracy is limited to the Christmas
Ocean, where the pirates can make it home for dinner with
their loot. The closer you sail to the red areas the more
likely you are to find yourself shorn of cash, clothing, electronics, and your lady's honor. Piracy in the Christmas
Ocean has become a way of life along the wilder shores of
cruising, assisted, alas, by the trusting nature of sailors and
a highly developed talent for corruption among the local
constabulary.

The Christmas Ocean has all the bad stuff. Who has
ever seen fog over a thousand fathoms? *Meltemis*, willi-
waws, and the like are generated by air falling down the
sides of mountains. Lightning is rare in the deep oceans as
are mosquitoes and flies and garbage and sewerage and
other reminders of our failing land-based ecosystems. True
you do have hurricanes and typhoons to deal with but,
with a bit of caution and a dollop of good planning, you
can sail for a lifetime and never even come close to one.
And if you should be caught in an ultimate storm, ask
yourself what you would rather have . . . a thousand feet
to lee or a thousand miles?

I will not try to catalog all of the difficulties posed for
the sailor in the Christmas Ocean. You will, too soon, discover them for yourself. So get quickly away from the
shore and always remember that in the Christmas Ocean,

as in life itself, the most danger always lies nearest to the mirage of safety.

On land more people have accidents in their bathtubs than anywhere else and at sea more sailors are lost within sight of land than ever were overwhelmed by the mythic horrors of the deep oceans.

CREW

While there exist ancient and accurate charts of the sea which tell in exquisite detail what you may expect in all the great oceans, after a thousand generations of humanity, there still are no guidelines to determine whether the sailing crew you are signing on be devils or angels.

In truth, you do not want either. Too good can be as exasperating as too bad. What is needed on a small boat over a long passage, is someone whose faults are mildly attractive and whose good qualities do not cause your own to suffer by comparison.

Acceptable crew is a vital part of your offshore adventure. It is unlikely that the sea itself will kill you, but it is very likely that a sour, petulant, and lazy watchmate can make you wish that you were dead. After elysian visions of passage, a belching, farting, snoring, lazy lout in the next bunk can turn dreams to dross. Trial passages tell you no more about the evil that lurks in the heart of crew than does your first impression. The bad stuff in them, and the good stuff also, appears, as if on schedule, five days out and five hundred miles downwind. Every crew member comes with a bundle of emotional problems, an aeolian box of miseries which you will get to open when it is too late to do anything about it. Since it has not been established that any one human being is really any better or any worse than any other, the only way to deal with crew is to admit that they are as bad as you are. Then you can deal with their foibles with as much forgiveness as you deal with your own. Since you have not been able to change yourself very much throughout your life, it is unlikely that you will be able to reform another person during the month or so that you will be together.

Before you get down to the business of acquiring crew, you must be most excruciatingly clear about the financial arrangements with them. There are three ways to go: paid crew, unpaid crew, and paying crew. All arrangements are full of problems but the only alternative to one of these three choices is to sail alone. Solo sailors maintain that they indulge in their lonely madness to avoid the bother of dealing with crew. In general, taking on crew carelessly is like marrying in haste. It can be followed by long periods of repentance.

With real sailors—and paid crew usually fall into that category—the great and overriding drive is the desire to be passaging. If you go with paid crew you may expect more of them than of unpaid crew, not because you are paying them, but because they are committed to the sea. If both you and your paid crew are competent skippers, there may be a trial of wills which, if not set right, can unsettle the passage. There can only be one skipper and that must be you.

Unpaid crew who will sail with you for food and fun only tend to be your emotional colleagues. They are out there for the adventure, the same as you are. Unpaid crew can be drawn from a larger sample than any other thus making it a bit more likely to match your needs and prejudices. They are, however, considerably less permanent, less reliable, and more likely to jump ship than paid crew.

There is crew who will pay you for the privilege of sailing. I have never known a good outcome from taking paying crew aboard. I once witnessed the arrival of a boat in the harbor of Galle in Sri Lanka. The anchor was no sooner in the water than the crew, all paying their way, erupted from the boat like dogs scattering from a skunk in their haste to be away. The divergence of the stories of the passage, from the skipper on one side and the crew on the other, would have been hilarious had the tellers not been in such emotional pain. Most of the complaints from the skipper were about a gluttonous, disobedient crew and from the crew about a parsimonious and drunken skipper.

In the long run, accidental acquisition is probably the best way to recruit. Cyndee did a bikini bounce down the dock in Panama and asked, all in one deep breath, if we were going to Tahiti and could she come along. All of our male chemicals aboard agreed without investigation or reservation. She came on board *sans* experience, *sans* reference, *sans* anything save a bosun's knife, bubbly enthusiasm, and bikini. She remained for five years, married my mate, and left with all passionately in love, not with her figure, but with the strength and the consistency of her spirit.

It was a high risk with a happy ending. I have tried listening to my chemistry on other occasions, rarely with such marvelous luck. But accidental acquisition is not a bad way to go. Most folk are fundamentally the same, so what you stumble over as you blindly grope about for crew the first time around is likely to be as good as what you might agonize over.

Recruiting friends is very, very dangerous. The guy with whom you have pleasantly played poker for years may have an *idée fixe* concerning the nature of your relationship that simply will not work at sea. The nifty gal liked by all may find that close confines and limited social contacts are different from being part of a larger crowd. It is better, far better, to develop a new relationship with crew at sea than to try to transmigrate to your boat relationships that have worked on land. And that goes for relatives too.

Should you find someone you really like but whose skills and experience are limited, take them on and teach them. You cannot change personality but you can share knowledge. In the final analysis a quieting, or disquieting, feeling in your belly is as good a bellwether as anything.

Avoid smokers, dopers and alcoholics. While many of your friends on land have habits that may amuse you or at least not repel you, contiguity and time ratchet up repugnance.

Having avoided smokers, dopers, and drunks you now must live with the choices that you have made. Any attempt to seriously change how a person acts and reacts is feckless and unrewarding. Even you, perhaps, cannot stop smoking and I, certainly, keep letting out my waistline. Why then should we expect that others, neither better nor worse than ourselves, could change their way of living for the sake of 30 days at sea. We all are made up of bundles of traits, some good and some bad. Some more and some less acceptable to a skipper choosing a crew. There can be no perfect crew so there will be no perfect choice. At best your crew will be no more perfect than you.

Once the seeking and the questioning is behind you, make a choice, and accept that choice fully. Those you choose deserve that you accept, without reservation, both them and the choice that you have made. If you have reservations about your choices the passage will be a disaster. Be determined that you will like and admire your crew and thus make it difficult and ungracious for your shipmates to disappoint your high hopes for them.

Unalloyed approval of crew is the ultimate method of assuring good passages. Disapproval always returns disapproval. Approval never does.

SKIPPERS

Every skipper has horror stories about crew. Some complain that the ultimate curse of sailing is the difficulty of acquiring acceptable crew. Not great crew, mind you, just acceptable crew. "Greedy, thieving, and lazy," are the favorite descriptions, followed, almost invariably by, "and they eat like horses."

It can be argued that good crew are hard to find. Skippers do have a legitimate gripe about quality and dedication and loyalty. But it is a two-way street. If a skipper wants quality and dedication and loyalty from a crew he must demonstrate his own quality, dedication, and loyalty to them. Most skippers do, but as this tale will tell, there are exceptions.

The other side of the coin of complaint, the crew's side, is rarely heard. Crew who have sailed with awful skippers are reluctant to discuss them or, more likely, nobody will listen. It is an ancient tradition of the sea that skippers have an armlock on the truth and the network to disseminate it. Crew come and go without a constituency of their own.

Oscar Wilde (who ought to have known) said that power degrades both those who use it and those on whom it is used. There is no place in human intercourse where the use and abuse of power is more easy to achieve than at sea. A skipper, any skipper, good, fair or lousy, is by fiat king of the hill.

Prefering those who are trod upon to those doing the trodding, I have appointed myself ombudsman to the crews of the world and have collected and verified some wild tales of skipperly deviation.

Generally bad skippers are just nasty, rarely violent. But Ziggy and his bride had the misfortune to ship with just such a man and twelve passengers (yes twelve!) on a 46-foot boat bound for Kenya from the Mediterranean.

The skipper, Neil, was about 60 and when sober was merely petty. When drunk, which he was not infrequently, he was violent and capable of putting his vessel, his crew, and himself in jeopardy.

Neil's favorite ploy was to require his crew to buy

their own food, cigarettes, and other supplies and then claim the supplies for the boat when, in fear and loathing, they signed off before the end of the passage.

Starting with 14 crew (all paying for their passage plus their consumables) the boat shed people all along the Mediterranean until, upon reaching Suez, only Ziggy and his wife were left of the original 14. The others gave up on Neil (and their money) after Neil tried to have them arrested in Malta on a trumped-up charge of mutiny.

The brouhaha started one afternoon when the boat lay becalmed. Neil was below in his cabin swilling the hooch and three of the crew went swimming. Neil came roaring up out of his cabin, truncheon in hand, and accused the swimmers of God knows what. Then he proceeded to beat them with his club.

A drunken 60-year old skipper, flailing about with a club at a young and strong crew, could easily find himself in the water, if not worse. Calm heads prevailed, the club was taken from Neil and he was escorted to his cabin to sober up. This was the basis for his charge of mutiny.

Upon reaching Malta, Neil jumped into the dinghy and pulled for shore. He went to the police with his tale and they, on only the strength of the skipper's word, came out to the boat and bundled the whole crew into the hoosegow. The Maltese police are not stupid and when they heard the other side of the story, the crew was released and Neil was fined for landing while under quarantine. He was then told to get out of Malta and never come back.

Most of the crew signed off in Malta and the rest in Italy. Only Ziggy, who had been promised plane fare back to Germany from Kenya, remained aboard and saw the boat, with her drunken captain, safely down the Red Sea. By the time the boat reached Djibouti, Neil was completely out of control and Ziggy, fearing that he and his bride would be abandoned in Kenya (as indeed he would have been), chose to take his chances of finding another vessel in Djibouti.

Neil was crewless in Djibouti, not unlike being eyeless in Gaza. It would be nice to report that justice was served and Neil was stuck. But, with the gift of gab of a sober drunk in trouble, he pulled off an unfair coup. The British Navy was in Djibouti for a few days and at a cocktail party aboard a cruiser he spun his tilted tale of woe. There was a buzz among the hosts and four British naval officers offered to sail with him down to Kenya. It seems that the Brits require that their young officers have some experience of small boat ocean sailing and the four were given time to make the passage to Kenya where their ship was due to call to pick them up. Neil's boat was completely re-supplied at the expense of Her Majesty and off went Neil in glee. Talk about luck for the bad guys!

None of us who knew the real story would rat on Neil although we were all sorely tempted. I hope the Brits did not regret the passage. It is perhaps a vain hope since much of the donated supplies clinked as they were swung aboard.

Tim is an elegant young man who signed as the crew of one on to a yacht skippered by a woman. The plan was to cruise the Mediterranean with Tim and his skipper woman to share all duties.

The problem that arose was sex. Most women skippers are professional types who keep their personal life separate and intact from emotional involvements. Women, being somewhat more human than men, make better, or at least more congenial skippers as a rule, but poor Tim fell into the hands of the screaming exception. His skipper, let us call her Sully, was 50 (seems young enough to me) and Tim was barely 22, so that when Sully suggested that one of Tim's duties was servicing the skipper as well as the boat, her invitation was turned down by Tim with ill-disguised, callow disgust. Tim was astounded that an 'old lady' would make such advances.

Tim had never heard Ol' Ben Franklin's argument that mistresses of somewhat advanced age are far superior to young ones. In rejecting her, admittedly indelicately, he raised the ire of Sully to the point where lust denied transmutes into ferocious need for revenge.

I can sympathize with Sully as a woman scorned but not as a skipper taking advantage of her power. The occasion when reprisal first appeared was upon Tim's return to the boat after an evening out. He went to his bunk in the fo'c's'le to find Sully, naked, awaiting him. He threw her out, unceremoniously, which is no way to deal with a naked lady. Her dignity in shreds, Sully reverted to the exercise of pure skipperly power.

Tim was allowed only the cheapest of food for the rest of the voyage. No canned goods, they were reserved for Sully. He was required to stand six hour watches against her three hour watches and, while she allowed herself the use of the autopilot, Tim was obliged to hand steer for his six hours. A major abuse was Sully's insistence that she accompany Tim on all of his shore trips thus short circuiting any of the normal conquests which sailors pursue as soon as they hit land. How was Tim to explain to the cute young thing in the bar the presence of a woman hanging on his arm old enough to be his mother? A devilish piece of business.

But Sully really gave Tim his comeuppance when the time came to sign off and get paid. Tim was due, by the terms of their agreement, $1,100. Sully, by dint of creative deductions, actually paid him $75. It had cost him $1,025 for refusing her charms.

She deducted most of what she owed him because, although they had finished the passage as Tim had agreed, the passage took a week less than she had expected. He did the work but at her reckoning he did not do it long enough.

There was a moment when Sully was on watch and she did not see a big ship bearing down on them. Tim was resting on the foredeck on a three-dollar cotton blanket and he leaped up and just managed to avoid a collision. In the melee the three-dollar blanket went overboard. In her gratitude for Tim having saved her boat she deducted $32 from his pay for the cheap blanket that he lost.

For three sea sickness patches, certainly an obligation of the boat, she charged him $24.

For hand cleaner after he worked on the engine, $5.

For letter paper and envelopes, $3.

For use of Sullys toothpaste for two days when his ran out, $3.

For soap, $2.

For laundering sheets and pillowcases, $33.

For notebook paper, $3.

And as the ultimate indignity Sully 'fined' Tim $55 for 'disobeying orders'. Lucky he wasn't keelhauled.

Maybe he should have slept with her.

WOMEN SAILORS

My own reaction to women was, I recognize, essentially priapic in origin. I was driven by the biblical exhortation to perform multiplication, as I suspect are all men.

These antediluvian prods and pricks are welcomed by us men as defining our proper place in the world.

I am troubled by these assigned roles, both those relegated to men and those to women, since in any grand scheme the special function of women is vastly more important than that of men. Men are, by accidental virtue of some raucous genes, merely the carriers of racial variety, while women are the bearers and the nurturers of the race itself.

Emerging from this is an idiosyncratic view of human history. At one time, in the chaotic mists of creation, females owned the world. They led, they ordered, and they designed our lives. They were worshiped and obeyed until one of them, more prescient than most, discovered that a considerable amount of her time and energy was taken up with war, politics and sports, thus diminishing the opportunities for birthing, nursing, and loving. She concluded that war, sports and politics, while amusing games, were hardly central. At that moment a vast conspiracy was born.

It did not require much argument to convince her female cohorts who, anyway, were deep involved in babies, moon, and blood, that an interesting bargain could easily be struck to their infinite advantage. Let us, she posited, hand over political and martial hegemony to the men who after insemination have little to do anyway, and we can get on undisturbed with our cosmic centrality.

And so it came about that women became the 'weaker' sex and men ruled the world.

Jenny came aboard for an Atlantic crossing as a somewhat bemused appendix to her week-old bridegroom. Brian had built himself a sailboat in which he tooled about on day sails off the southern coast of England. His dream, his central reason for being, was to do a circumnavigation with his new bride. When they joined us, he was gung-ho and she was not quite certain upon what she was embarking.

The gung lasted until the first dawning when Brian turned green. Stick-on patches, copper bracelets and pills did no good and poor Brian weakened steadily for the entire 28-day passage. Meanwhile Jenny grew stronger each day. In the rolly-polly of the passage she could read, sew and knit, loved to go below to do galley duty, and baked our bread for the passage. She handled sails, worked the foredeck and, as a blessed bonus rarely found in either male or female crew, chatted only when chatted at. She became that most precious of shipmates, an amiable, amenable, effective and silent sailor.

As Brian's dream of distant fabled seas evaporated in nausea, we could see a small cloud looming on the horizon of their marriage. She, not he, was the sailor. She, not he, had a circumnavigation in her future.

Gloria had come aboard at the launching of UNLIKELY VII in Miami. Her sailing credits were as limited as her spirit was not. Coming through the Yucátan Channel, currents and winds collided heaping up seas through which we could see the noonday sun. I simply could not summon the discipline to stand at the wheel and watch as the monsters roared down upon us. All I wanted to do was cower below, out of sound and sight of this watery Armageddon.

Gloria kissed my forehead, murmured "poor baby," and steered through the maelstrom right on into Cozumel. Actually she did not steer, she danced to the seas, charming them with a sinuous sexiness and, when they got too boisterous, she deployed those little tricks from up her sleeve which women have used to control importunate folk since the beginning of time.

Marilyn had never set foot on a sailboat when I phoned her from Senegal. I needed a companion to cross the Atlantic in my 32 footer and knowing her to be accommodating and decorative, I invited her to come along. Accommodating, yes. Decorative, yes, but packed into that small and delicious frame was a will that kept this tyro of a skipper going through bad seas and ignorance.

We were three aboard, actually four since Marilyn doubled often at the wheel and always in the galley. As the seas piled up her eyes widened in disbelief but never a word of dismay or recrimination.

I knew I had a winner when, on her first dark and windy night at sea, the moon surged out from clouds behind her with the intensity of a searchlight from hell. Although she was terrified to turn and see what the infernal brightness might be, she stood her paralyzed ground, never giving way to the terrors she must have felt.

And then the scenario screamed into the improbable as an invisible flying fish thrust from a white-capped sea came aboard and slapped her across her face. I would have fainted. She did not.

Subsequently, she married me in spite of knowing that

she would certainly be required to double not only at the wheel and in the galley but in my life itself.

Given the few months's advantage that a husband has over his wife in sailing experience, any woman can overcome the 'handicap' of being beautiful, small, slightly softer, and considerably more human.

There are more and more women skippers out there sailing their own boats each year. They are, on some kind of average, better sailors than men. They are sailors because they want to sail.

Women have too long been culturally handicapped by the fiction that "sailing is not for ladies." Too many women live lives defined for them and not what they might freely choose for themselves. Ultimately, that is what keeps women from the sea. The real handicap of being female is the ease with which she accepts the oppressive hegemony of men.

If a man wishes to sail with his woman he must help her to confront, head on, not the sea (which she can handle very well by herself) but the male imposed sense of female inadequacy. She must know that there is nothing aboard a sailing vessel that a man can do that she cannot do as well and there are some things she can do a lot better.

It is the skipper's primary obligation to disenchant her of any feeling of incompetence by forcing upon her all of the tasks that happen aboard. She must learn the sea and the vessel, as he did, by the doing. She must know that nothing is beyond her abilities and that his Olympian command of the boat and the sea rests, in most cases, on a mere few months more of hands-on experience than she has had.

Most importantly of all she must be at the wheel while entering and leaving port for all of his colleagues to see. She must stand tall at the wheel, issuing unnecessarily loud orders, which seems to be what men like best about sailing. She, given just a bit of practice, will issue orders just as good and in a much quieter way.

While he was playing boat, she was busy rearing his children. She will learn to play boat more responsibly than he does. Were she not responsible the species would not survive. That same sense of responsibility, brought to the sea, will guarantee continuation of the passage.

When it comes to sailing a small boat on a long off-shore passage, being female is a curable handicap. The medicine is simple, honest concern. The doctor is the skipper to whom she has mysteriously and lovingly bonded herself not only as crew but as lifemate.

THE WELCOMER

Every sailor knows him. He's the guy at the end of the pier who happens to be idling about when you pull into Tahiti or Naha or Kobe or Manila or any other port in a sailor's world.

"Welcome to Papeete." (or Tel Aviv or Hurghada or Bueneventura or Oyster Bay or you name it.) "Welcome, welcome. Hope you had a fine passage."

How nice of this fine, usually grizzled fellow to be there just as you arrive and how reassuring is his obvious pleasure in your visit to his port. A real sailor's welcome, from one crosser of oceans to a newcomer, a traveler tired and hungry for a human touch and directions to the nearest bakery.

"Just admiring the sunset and yearning to be back out there again when I saw your fine yacht sail in. What is she, Swedish built? Taiwan you say? You could have fooled me. She looks like a Rassy to me. Well those fellows in the East have certainly come a long way.

"Have you cleared yet? No problem. I'll just have a word with the harbormaster, sort of a cousin of mine, and have you all sorted out in a jiffy. No problem, no problem.

I have nothing pressing on for a bit and I'll be glad to help. Back in a sec.

"Damn. My cousin seems to be off to a wedding (or funeral or party or bar mitzvah), he'll be away for a few hours. Sorry, I wish I could help.

"Electrical problems? Don't we all. Sometimes I feel like dumping the whole kit overboard and back to good old kerosene. But what seems to be wrong?

"Well now, isn't that a coincidence. My brother-in-law is the resident expert in alternators. Takes 'em apart and puts 'em together blindfolded, he does. But busy, busy all the time. Don't rightly know if I could drag him all the way down here. But he'd be your boy if we could get him. Expensive? Not for any friend of mine he isn't. He owes me, he does.

"Look I'll grab a taxi and see if he's free. No, never mind the cab fare, it's my pleasure. Now really you must not insist and anyway you've given me too much. I'll give you the change when I get back. Shame though about this ten dollar bill. Pity to waste it on a cabbie. Why, I can get you 30% over bank rate if you have a bit more to change. Maybe tomorrow I'll take you out to the 'market'. You know, just a littlest bit black. Nah, never had any problem with the cops. Related to most of them. Anyway till to-morrow. Don't dare pay for anything with dollars. Just a waste. Here take a loan of some francs (or dinars or shekels or liras) to tide you over. Just you save those won-derful dollars.

"Want me to pick up some vittles on the way? You must be dying for a piece of bread or how about a couple of cold beers? Huh? Doesn't that sound good? I'll see what's around that I can buy cheap. No problem, I'll be right back.

"Long as I'm going I think I'll scout up my uncle. Whizz of a mechanic: that engine of yours did sound a tiny bit wheezy. He'll have it right in a jiffy.

"Don't listen to too much talk around the dock. They're mostly commission men. You know, sort of touts who double the price and get a kickback. Bums mostly. Try like hell to look like real sailors. Makes you laugh to hear them talk.

"Tell you what. You know the sort of place this is . . . a little baksheesh always helps but you got to be damned sure you're giving to the right people. Suppose I just spread some of my money around for you. Straighten out with you later. Naturally my brother-in-law the harbormaster won't take a dime.

"What? That's what I said. My cousin the harbormaster. Must have misheard me. My funny accent I guess. Anyway he will keep everybody else from being too greedy.

"My name is Nachum (or Nimrod or Hans or Stanislaw). Everybody knows me around here. Retired some years ago. Made my pile in the market. What? Ha! Ha! No, not that market, the other one, the legit one. Not rich but comfortable. Got enough to help out a fellow sailor now and then.

"Well okay, I'll take the dollars since you can't leave the boat. Promise I'll get you a rate you won't believe. Don't spread the news around though. Don't want to spoil a good thing. How do I do it? Well listen, it just so happens the bank manager is my wife's father and they can do things with money you won't believe. Not for everyone though, just in the family.

"See you later. Mind don't listen to the idlers. Those bums will say anything to get a commission. See you soon."

And off he goes with your 500 greenbacks tucked into his pocket and before you can even get your sails stowed he's back with a small platoon of horny handed, hail fellows just oozing with the need to fix every problem you ever had and a truckload of supplies that you might recall just making some price inquiries about.

"Couldn't resist this stuff. What a bargain. Sort of fell off the back of a truck if you know what I mean. Thought I might as well do you a favor and give you first shot at the whole deal. Keep you in feed for a month it will. Meet my cousin, uncle, brother-in-law, wife's father. Just let them loose. They are all magicians. Cost? Almost nothing . . . like you are almost in the family. Right?

"Here count the money. How do you like that rate. Better than I told you. Much better and all brand new crisp bills, not the junk they try to pass you at the bank, all torn and dirty."

With that, the 'family' proceeds to take your boat apart and their kids start heaving aboard more food than you can possibly stow. The repair bills are settled after much banging and hammering and explanations that the "stuff left over just slowed your old engine down. She'll go much better now."

Naturally everyone wants to get paid in greenbacks. None will touch the crisp new bills that you got such a great rate on, and finally everyone is paid and the victualing is completed, and you sink back onto your now quiet boat clutching the $2000 worth of pounds (or pesos or yens or God knows what) that you could simply not resist changing at that terrific rate. And off to sleepy bye.

Next day the engine absolutely refuses to start. The alternators seem to be burned out and the batteries are dead. Your stove blows up when you light it for breakfast and your autopilot, which had a slight sniffle before the invasion, has died of double pneumonia. The fridge is as warm as your temper and no one in the whole marina has heard of your helpful sailor. And lot of expensive gear seems to be temporarily, at least you hope, mislaid and the thought of explaining all this to the police is just too embarrassing.

Oh well, even with all the damage you are cozened by the wonderful rate on the local currency you got for your dollars, a feeling that lasts just until the first time you try to spend some.

So the next time you pull into a strange port and our friend hails you with a "Welcome!" don't even let him get a second 'welcome' out. Throw him instantly overboard. Do not worry about his drowning. It is impossible, buoyed up as he is by his own hot air and all those other suckers' money.

FIDDLER'S GREEN

Tris looked down at his ruined body and declared, "Shit, enough of this crap." He turned to the lithe, young boy standing by his bed in a Thai hospital. "You earned it, lad, might as well be yours and to hell with the tax goonies. Take it and lam on out of these waters. Get yourself over to Bombay. Tie up at the Gate of India and make one more trip for me to Soukilaki Street. Have one more loverly pipe and raise it to old Tris."

Thus Tris parted with the weird craft, part sailboat part rehab room, named, after he had his first amputation and with all of the bitterness he could muster, OUTWARD LEG.

Tris didn't own the boat. It was loaned to him by a rich Australian probably paying penance for past sins. The Aussie was to get it back but Tris, when he was about to go, chuckled over the inability of ordinary folk to "take it with them." Tris took with him, when he went, all of the debts he had accumulated through beggary and bombast in his long life of making luckier folk feel sorry for him.

So young Chan leaned over Tris and gently kissed his cheek. Tris was so far along in his final passage that he hardly felt the kiss. The young Thai lad boarded OUTWARD LEG as Tris had directed and sailed off toward India where no one gives much of a damn about such niceties as ownership or papers. When the boat fetched up at the Gate of India, that crumbling memory of the dead Raj, OUTWARD LEG bore a new name, FRGEM, a silent doff in memory of Tris's response to anyone who stood in his crippled way.

"Frig the bastards, Chan, frig 'em arsewise and bury them deep in the shit they dump on me." Tris would fume. Chan excised an 'i' and had his own chuckle, a technique he learned from Tris, at the expense of the universe.

So exits Chan, obediently lost in the delights of Sukilaki Street.

Tris lived hard but died easy. He had used up all of the pain and indignity that most of us save for our last moments in his everyday business of keeping barely alive. Each man, he would opine, is issued, like orgasms, a finite measure of pain at birth to be used up in life or husbanded for penultimate moments. When Tris's passed over the bar it was, compared to lost limbs and afflictions and angina, a piece of cake. Whatever awaited him, oblivion or the delights of heaven or even the tortures of hell, would, he breathed quietly as he breathed his last, "be better than the muck they fed me here."

A slight greenish haze greeted him as he opened his eyes. All was a bit out of focus and wavy like the sheen on moire silk. Not unpleasant, indeed soothing and restful. There was, for the first time in decades, not a single pain in his body.

As he glanced down, he discovered the wiggly pleasure he was feeling was from his ten lost toes, attached to healthy feet and so on up to fill out legs that had long since "been snatched" from him.

"I be damned. Wherever I am I am better than anywhere I ever was. Ten toes and two legs. Wonder what price the bastards will extort for this development?" But he knew . . . knew at that moment without doubt or fear that his price had already been paid in the long agony of just staying alive. He was getting his comeuppance, whatever the price, and, contrary to most, his comeuppance felt wonderful.

Someone laid a hand on Tris's shoulder and through the pleasant wavy blue said, "I have my two hundred miles' day. Got it just before I jibed over. What's yours to be, lad?"

Tris raised his eyes from his feet and without much thinking about it blurted, "Can I stand on the bloody things?"

Chichester, for that is who it was, laughed and pulled Tris up onto his new found feet. "Stand, walk, dance, wiggle and flex. Any damned thing you please although it seems a mighty small ultimate request," and then thoughtfully, "but I guess that's because I always had mine."

Still not looking beyond the miracle of being made whole Tris missed the group of wavery, watery beings who clustered chattering in a thousand accents and tongues, all of which Tris inexplicably understood.

"Anybody you want to speak to? Noah, Leif the Lucky, Eric the Red, Columbus, Magellan, Vasco da Gama, Ponce de León, Sir Francis Drake, Lord Nelson. John Paul Jones, Farragut, George Dewey, Jean Lafitte, Amundsen, Perry, Ted Turner," Chichester asked. "Anybody at all?"

Bemused and uncertain about where he was Tris said, "Anybody but Ted." Then as he reached blearily for a familiar and comfortable friend, "How about Henry?"

"Sorry he didn't, oops, might not make it." Chichester said. "Is he a sailor or just a bookseller?"

"Only sailors here?"

"Only real sailors here."

"Where am I, why is everybody floaty, how the bloody hell am I standing here on two new legs and talking to you who be dead these decades?"

"Well now lad . . . you are dead too. I guess I better run you through the ship so to speak, get you acquainted with your reward, your sailor's reward."

"Damn better well better," snapped Tris, who for being dead, had lost little of his bite. "Let's get on with it. I am not in heaven, since it seems to me that good folk, not only sailors, are entitled to heaven. I am not in hell 'cause I feel too good and there are them feet! So where am I and who are all those becostumed, bewigged, and bedraggled folk twittering about?"

Chichester, in a voice that promised a better life than Tris had ever known said, "Tristan, you are in Fiddler's Green."

"Bloody hell! Fiddler's Green be it? Thought that was a fairy tale. Let's see now, Fiddler's Green, where every sailor is supposed to go, be he good or evil, as his just reward for simply being a sailor."

"That be it, lad, that be it and you are here and this is no fairy tale," said Chichester.

"But why, why would the glory man, whoever he is, favor sailors, good or evil, over the rest of the mob. Why?"

"Thousand answers to that poser." Chichester chuckled. "How about, for starters, sailors are the only really free folk? How about the light hand they lay on the earth? How about the lift they give the mob as they head out for far horizons? How about new continents discovered? How about the reward for simply pitting their bare hands and given minds against His seas and winds? How's that for starters?"

"Be there more?"

"Sure. Closer to home, how about payback to those who transport the stick-in-the-mud mob on the wordy wings of adventure? How about making ordinary folk feel bigger than life?

" You mean He read my little efforts and that is why I'm here?"

"Not only. If you had never taken a pen to paper your sailorly life would have been enough."

"But not all I wrote was, well, exactly true. What about that?"

"That is not important. People thought all was as noted and it uplifted them. You are in Fiddler's Green: no sin, no absolution, no retribution. You are what you are, a sailorman and that's enough."

"I am what I am," and Tris added as a bemused afterthought, "is the spinach eater here too?"

"Maybe, I don't know, but he's a sailor, isn't he."

The legend of Fiddler's Green is as old as navigation of the seas. It has been known by various names down through the centuries: The Great Ship, Davey Jones' Locker, etc. All captains and all sailors, great and small pass on to Fiddler's Green.

Phoenician galleys, Roman triremes, Viking ships, sailing ships, frigates, battleships, destroyers, cruisers, submarines, aircraft carriers—all are included. A countless host of maritime heroes of all the wars are there along with all the sailors of discovery as well as anyone who ever consigned himself to the mysteries of the oceans.

Old sailors never die, they just slip their last cable and wake up in Fiddler's Green.

IMMIGRANTS TO THE SEA

There were three of us in the room wearing sweaters. Two had ties under their blue V necks and I had an open collar under my orange crew neck sweater. The rest of the hundred and fifty men all wore blue blazers, double breasted, sewn and braided in gold and cuffed with golden buttons engraved with anchors, intertwined line, and other marine designs. Some of the buttons were, I am sure, of real gold as were the majority of the folk in the room; solid as the 14K they sported. Neckties were scattered with flying fish and trousers were of varying shades of unobtrusive colors save for one gent, saltier than the rest, who sported a pair of bright red slacks.

The men were well fed and over fifty. Their women were beautiful and tough looking, managing to meld attractiveness and money into an ageless sexuality.

The occasion was a Mystic Seaport meeting of a sailing club of ancient lineage and unassailable respectability. I squirmed in my sweater and was relieved when the house lights dimmed and our lecturer tickled our history bone with an erudite and amusing retailing of the origins and growth of our 'pastime', as he called sailing.

I settled back secure that I knew these folk. No surprises here and if I was a bit *outré* for their tastes it was better that I should attract the small smiles than the two regulars in the blue sweaters who, unlike myself, should have known better.

The first crack in the facade almost swept past me. The podium was dealing with the recent history of the America's Cup and their shenanigans with the New Zealanders. In this heavy ambience of the New York Yacht Club dragged north, I knew with certainty what was coming. That is, I thought I knew for, without warning and out of context, the speaker announced that, "as a Calvinist, I view the recent defense of the Cup much as I would a mugging on the streets of New York."

I thought that either he had misspoken or I had misheard, so secure was I in my prejudgment. But as he went on to reduce the Cup's defense to an arrogant farce, I had to reconsider my opinions, first of the speaker and later, on other evidence, of the sea of blue about me.

Afterwards the meeting settled back with genteel chitchat and good fellowship. Surprising events behind me, I was once again secure in the regularity of these blue jacketed and Laura Ashley-ed folk until, as we passed from meeting to cocktails, one of the ladies greeted a friend with, "My dear, I hardly recognized you with your clothes on!"

This one remark, so out of phase with the surface proprieties of the meeting, instantly evoked the strange

sailorly folk with whom I, and I hope you, have been con-
sorting for some decades and who are recalled in this
book. The cruising types I have met fit no mold but share
one clear characteristic: all have come to recognize that
real freedom from our too-much-with-us world exists only
at sea. We are all, with a wink at the blue jackets who understand anyway, anarchists and revolutionaries. While
we carry no bombs, indeed some will not even carry a pop
gun, many countries consider us freedom seekers as dangerous as old time Bolsheviks.

No matter from what huge trove, or absence, of
money, or how noble our lineage, we are all strangely
equal in each other's eyes. We are all immigrants to the
sea. Each of us starts from ground zero and gains sailorly
respect, not from what we bring to the sea but from what
we learn from the sea. We are the only real democracy left
on earth.